WHAT
EVERY
RADICAL
SHOULD
KNOW
ABOUT
STATE
REPRESSION

WHAT EVERY RADICAL SHOULD KNOW ABOUT STATE REPRESSION

a guide for activists

Victor Serge

foreword by Anthony Arnove

introduction by Dalia Hashad

SEVEN STORIES PRESS

new york • oakland • london

Seven Stories Press
140 Watts Street
New York, NY 10013
www.sevenstories.com

Library of Congress Cataloging-in-Publication Data is on file.

ISBN: 978-1-64421-367-4 (paperback)
ISBN: 978-1-64421-368-1 (ebook)

Printed in the USA

9 8 7 6 5 4 3 2 1

contents

2. The problem of illegality

3. Simple advice to revolutionaries

4. The problem of revolutionary repression

foreword

Anthony Arnove

Anyone setting out to confront injustice must contend with the contours of state repression and how to resist it. This is as true today as it was when Victor Serge (1890–1947, born Victor Lvovich Kibalchich) wrote this trenchant book, first published in France in 1925 under the title *Les coulisses d'une sûreté générale: ce que tout révolutionnaire devrait savoir sur la répression.*

What Every Radical Should Know about State Repression (the original English title was *What Everyone Should Know about Repression*) emerged from Serge's work with the Communist International (Comintern), also known as the Third International, after it formed in March 1919. Recently forcibly exiled from France after several years of imprisonment there for his revolutionary activities, Serge threw himself into political activity in revolutionary Russia and joined the Bolshevik Party in May 1919.

As Susan Weissman writes in her indispensable political biography of Serge, *Victor Serge: The Course Is Set on Hope*, "Serge took part in the first three Congresses of the Comintern, . . . met the leaders of the international revolutionary movements, . . . and like all his comrades performed a host of functions." One of these was as "commissar in charge of the archives of the old Ministry of the Interior, the Okhrana." The Okhrana was the extremely repressive Department for Defense of Public Security and Order, which operated from 1881 to 1917 and deployed extensive police powers to suppress popular movements in the Russian empire. These archives gave Serge a richly documented understanding of the tools of state repression, including surveillance, spying, infiltration, disinformation, and provocation.

During the civil war period, with the Russian Revolution under serious threat from the White army and multiple invading foreign powers, Weissman notes, Serge "worried that if . . . [Petrograd] fell the archives of the Okhrana would fall again into the hands of reactionaries, proving 'precious weapons for tomorrow's hangmen and firing-squads.' Serge saw to it that the archives were packed in boxes and ready to be smuggled out or burned at the last moment."

These archives would prove critical to his publication in 1921 in France of a series of articles for *Bulletin Communiste*, which became the basis of *Ce que tout révolutionnaire devrait savoir sur la répression*. They also informed his thinking about the thorny question of which institutions the Bolsheviks in Russia and other socialists would need in order to defend the gains of the revolution from counterrevolutionary forces intent on overthrowing the workers' revolution and preventing workers from taking power elsewhere.

While circumstances have changed, and some specifics of Serge's argument may seem dated to contemporary readers, we have a great deal to learn from his method in approaching these questions.

It was only moments ago in the history of the United States that the Federal Bureau of Investigation (FBI) systematically targeted and worked to disrupt the work of Martin Luther King, Jr. And it is impossible to understand the modern left without studying the profound damage done to Black, Puerto Rican, Indigenous, and other radical organizations by COINTELPRO.

In response to protests in Ferguson, Missouri, and elsewhere under the banner of the Movement for Black Lives, the US government directly targeted what it called "Black Identity Extremists."

Peace groups, Islamic cultural and religious centers, anti-death penalty organizations, and environmental justice collectives have been infiltrated, surveilled, and disrupted. In other cases, we have seen government provocateurs posing as activists engage in actions meant to discredit movements or to entrap people in adventurist plans concocted by the government to discredit organizers.

More commonly, at almost any demonstration one is likely to encounter self-negating "free speech zones," where activists are kettled in and prevented from freely assembling and expressing their views. Police routinely use violent methods to suppress protest and have in other cases effectively deputized vigilantes to act as their surrogates to attack demonstrators, and in some cases, even kill them. Some states have passed legislation to protect drivers who use their cars as weapons against protestors.

The fundamental reality underlying all these examples is that the state is not a neutral body. The police are not impartial enforcers of the rule of law. The state and the police serve very specific class interests and use their monopoly on legitimate violence to protect those interests, private property, and the smooth functioning of capitalism. That is, they use various forms of repression, including physical violence, to defend the institutional violence of capitalism.

"In every country," Serge writes in this volume, "the workers' movement had to win, in over half a century of struggle, the right to associate and the right to strike. . . . In the conflicts between capital and labor, the army has often intervened against labor—never against capital."

The state uses even greater violence globally to defend access to markets, vital resources, and exploitable labor; suppress popular uprisings; defend dictators who are vital to perceived national interests; and destabilize regimes that it cannot (or can no longer) control.

How we understand these questions is not only important in times of revolutionary upheaval or crisis, such as the period when this book was originally written, the aftermath of the Russian Revolution in 1917. Our understanding of these questions is critical for everyone who wishes to see a changed world. The great abolitionist Frederick Douglass (c. 1818–1895) explained why: "Power concedes nothing without a demand. It never did and it never will."

Serge understood this. In this short book, he sought to arm revolutionaries (as the original French subtitle described his intended readers) with an understanding of the methods of state repression, especially "surveillance, informing and provocation."

Serge's hope was that activists "will perhaps suffer fewer losses if given good warning of the means the enemy has at his disposal. There is thus good basis for practical reasons to study the main instrument of all reaction and all repression, that is, the apparatus for strangling all healthy revolt known as the police."

He viewed his motivation not just as an exposé of police misconduct but as "preparation . . . of the creative work of tomorrow." Serge rightly saw a connection between learning "the means the enemy has at his disposal" and genuinely understanding "the full extent of our own tasks."

Serge observes that many activists "forget the most elementary precautions" against surveillance and infiltration. This is a critical reminder, especially considering the myriad ways surveillance and repressive tools available to the police have increased radically since Serge's time.

Yet he cautions us, "Be on guard also against the tiresome mania for seeing an informer in every passerby," and urges us to be alert to the threat of "dilletantes and adventurers . . . taken by the idea of danger, intrigue, conspiracy."

Referring to the French revolutionary Louis Auguste Blanqui (1805–1881), Serge also rejects the methods of small adventurist organizations that act without accountability, often based on the theory that such actions will "awaken" the "sleeping" masses: "Communists do not prepare the insurrection the same way as the Blanquists . . . small groups of conspirators, led by a few intelligent, energetic idealists."

One of the greatest dangers of state repression is its chilling effect, when people choose not to act for fear of the consequences, Serge notes. "Repression can really only live off fear," he writes. "It would . . . be wrong to let oneself be taken in by the apparently perfect mechanism of czarist security." The Russian Revolution shows, in fact, how quickly genuinely popular forces can overcome such seemingly invincible powers.

If one does find oneself in an encounter with the police, Serge has important words that we would all do well to keep in mind. "Don't reply to any [police] question without having a defense counsel present. . . . Explaining yourself is dangerous; you are in the hands of professionals able to get something out of your every word." In addition, "Lying is extremely dangerous: it is difficult to construct a story without its defects being too obvious." And "don't try to be cleverer than them: the relationship of forces is too unequal for that."

There are two elements of Serge's polemic here on which his own thinking evolved, especially with the degeneration of the Russian Revolution and the failure of revolutions in Germany and elsewhere, which helped contribute to the rise of fascism in Europe.

Writing in the mid-1920s in vigorous defense of the Russian Revolution, Serge asserts with bravado, "the revolution is invincible." But he soon came to appreciate that, tragically, this was false. Russia was isolated and the Stalinist counterrevolution consolidated a new form of repressive state power in the Soviet Union, one that would target Serge himself and many of his comrades.

In the concluding section, "The Problem of Revolutionary Repression," Serge fails to understand, as he would later, the complex ways in which making a virtue of necessity in the civil war period, when the newly formed Bolshevik government was seeking to preserve the gains of the revolution against foreign powers and the White Terror, in fact planted seeds that would prove very fertile for the Stalinist consolidation of power.

Serge is right when he asserts that "the building of the

new society — which will be without prisons — does not begin with the construction of ideal prisons" and when he says the violence of the Bolsheviks cannot be equated with the violence of czarism or the armies seeking to crush the revolution. Following Vladimir Lenin (1870–1924) and Karl Marx (1818–1883), he stressed that "the workers' state works for its own disappearance," in stark contrast to the capitalist state. Yet he is too categorical in claiming that "the revolution does not have a choice of weapons" and "must be harsh." And overly teleological when he says, "Repression is effective when it acts along the lines of historical development."

Serge's later writings on Stalinism discredit the idea that "the essential features of the soviet state [were] not changed by" the repressive measures it had to take to defend the revolution. These later texts by Serge, such as *Memoirs of a Revolutionary* and *From Lenin to Stalin*, as well as those of Leon Trotsky (1879–1940) on Stalinism, should be read closely alongside this volume.

These are vital questions to debate today as we face a resurgent threat of fascism, a growing backlash against the past gains of civil rights struggles, heightened enforcement of literal and figurative borders, global environmental crises, and new police powers globally. We need to find ways to confront state power that are smart, effective, collective, democratic, inclusive, and revolutionary. And in doing this work, we have much to learn from the past experiences of other revolutionaries, especially Victor Serge.

Anthony Arnove
Hopwell, NJ, February 29, 2024

introduction to the 2005 edition
Dalia Hashad

Last year, a friend and I were lamenting the lack of popular revolt at the current political situation in the United States. Government policies and practices changed drastically, significantly curtailing individual rights, but our citizenry remained largely complacent. As an example of how bad things have become, the government has asserted the power to hold any person, citizen or not, in indefinite detention, without access to the courts, without ever seeing a lawyer, their families, their friends or the press. For a so-called "enemy combatant" there is no trial, no hearing and no chance to challenge the charges or to even hear the charges at all, if they in fact exist. The president just has to point his finger at any person and they disappear, perhaps forever, into a legal black hole. He was holding hundreds of people in Guantánamo Bay and three on US soil in this manner. This is a "democratic" government, gone wild with power.

What is more surprising than the fact that the government had assumed the authority to jail anyone, indefinitely, without any semblance of due process, is the conspicuous absence of popular revolt at this shocking usurpation of power. While some organizations publicly register their dismay and people grumble about the unfairness at dinner parties, where is the mass outrage? Any one of us could now disappear, without a reason, without recourse, at the hands of our government.

My friend shook his head, noting, "If all the McDonalds were shut down for one week, people would be in the streets in five minutes screaming about freedom. So few people actually get what's happening. The rest are just sleeping. We have got to wake some folks up!" I realized that current events were retracing familiar patterns. Historically, fundamental change often begins with people on the margins shaking the heart of society into wakeful consciousness. There is a way. People have been here before.

Victor Serge saw a central role for those who lived and thought on the margins. Giving me something to think about, he rejected the idea of a separateness of individuals, arguing "society has no fringe . . . no one is ever outside it, even in the depth of dungeons."[1] In his lifetime, Serge saw his share of dungeons — figurative and literal. From birth, his radical parents and humble surroundings conspired to create in him an indefatigable revolutionary for whom it was self-evident that his life's duty was "to ally [himself] with the exploited, and to work for the destruction of an intolerable system."[2] His parents escaped czarist dictatorship and oppression in Russia and settled in Brussels, where Serge was born in 1890. He grew up in abject poverty, losing a brother to malnutrition.

His father, himself a scholar, detested the school system but encouraged learning. Serge became a student without a school, pursuing education in his father's many books and with friends with whom he would digest and dissect ideas and theories. Seeking political reform, he immersed himself in diverse philosophies and carefully developed his own inspired ideas to which he devoted his life and which are woven throughout *What Every Radical Should Know About State Repression*. He learned early on that life "means, 'Thou shalt think, thou shalt struggle, thou shalt be hungry'." And perhaps more importantly, seemingly from the beginning, Serge was born with an irrepressible compulsion to obey an inner voice that instructed him: "Thou shalt fight back."[3]

"In setting 'the course on hope'," writes Serge's biographer Susan Weissman, "he pursued truth, struggled against privilege, and sought social justice and dignity. He chose to participate in the making of history by involving himself in the daily struggles of ordinary people. In Serge's time, these struggles were heroic."[4]

At great personal cost, Serge devoted his life to fighting back. Openly critical of authoritarianism and any manner of fascism, he spent more than a decade in various prisons, persecuted for his thoughts. As a man who translated his words into direct action, Serge's activism for political reform was his single, lifetime career that took many forms: he was an editor, activist, poet, prisoner, machine gunner, commissar, historian, pamphleteer, novelist, writer, political commentator, translator and always, always a revolutionary. In his own words, Serge "sought to harness together personal transformation and revolutionary action, in accordance with the motto of Elisée Reclus: 'As long as social injustice lasts we shall remain in a state of permanent revolution'."[5] And for his lifetime, he did.

I have always been particularly moved by stories of marginalized individuals seeking political reform. Zapatistas fighting for dignity in the mountains of Chiapas, Palestinians refusing to surrender dignity to colonial occupation, and the muted, lesser-known struggles of people quietly plugging away for political change, all capture my attention. They are emblematic of a process whose foundation is often slowly constructed over the course of patient years. They are people who want what every human being wants: freedom and fairness, however they perceive it.

Recently, I've been consumed by the struggle in my own country. In the United States, the past few years mark a historic period that few people anticipated. It is no longer safe to express your political opinion. Just last month, I provided legal services to a man visited at his home by the FBI who demanded an interview because he was critical of US foreign policy in the Middle East. Justified by the events of September 11, 2001, it was one of hundreds of cases I deal with in the widespread disintegration of civil liberties.

Historical perspective is often lost under the weight of the current resistance. Reading Serge is a comforting reminder that the struggle against various forms of repression is an ongoing one, fought over the entire course of history. Realizing that the search for a better political system is timeless, we can draw on the past, to fight our way through this dark period to something better. It is, at the same time, chilling and reassuring to read *What Every Radical Should Know About State Repression*. Written almost eighty years ago, it mirrors our present situation.

Using the threat of "terrorism" as cover, the US government assumed unchecked powers and adopted draconian policy emblematic of totalitarian governments. The rapid crumbling of laws that took place over months and short years was accompanied by the erection of a new "evil." US government policy, simplistically painting Muslims and Arabs as inherently wicked, paved the way for a strong resurgence of secret arrests and detentions, the use of torture as a tool of interrogation, the creation of a spy network, unchecked government surveillance and the widespread suppression of dissent—all discussed at length in Serge's text.

Serge's broad discussion on oft-recycled tools of state repression is as relevant today as it was yesterday. Upon reading Serge's section on police used to infiltrate and disrupt resistance groups, I immediately recalled the California policeman, Aaron Kilner, who took a false name to infiltrate a peace group two years ago. His identity was revealed only after he died in a motorcycle accident and members of the peace group read his obituary, accompanied with photograph, in the newspaper.

When I finished reading Serge's examination of government external surveillance of "suspicious" individuals, I reread a recent newspaper article about the US administration's latest initiative to conduct "external—even obvious" surveillance of individuals suspected of being "sympathetic to terrorists." Accordingly, the FBI has been chasing Muslims, Arabs and environmentalists. The placement of informers among prisoners reminds me of reports I've had from individuals in the criminal justice system who have been blackmailed into spying for law enforcement. The government's plan to use average citizens as agents to spy on people, the use of torture and the collection of information on private individuals are all discussed in Serge's text. The table of contents reads like a list of present-day offenses committed by the US administration.

The current administration has, no doubt, learned a thing

or two from other repressive governments. They are recycling, not inventing, many of these techniques. Things have happened here that US citizens only believe occur in other countries. After 9/11, the United States has violated both the law and the fundamental moral responsibility of any state by rounding up, detaining and deporting Muslim and Arab men, not because they had any connection to terrorist activity, but because they had the wrong religion or came from the wrong country. Even when there was no evidence that people had engaged in criminal activity, the government that held itself out as an international beacon of democratic due process secretly detained and summarily deported men because of their religion. In the middle of the night, FBI and immigration agents burst through doors and dragged people from their beds, terrifying families, neighborhoods and communities. No one could understand why and how people were being targeted or who might be the next to disappear into federal custody. At a recent public hearing, some victims of government repression told their stories. One young Syrian-American woman told of her family's experience with an early-morning raid in Seattle, Washington:

> At 6 o'clock in the morning about 15 police banged on our door. I was in my bedroom, asleep. I got up, and I'm standing in the hallway with the lights off. I keep hearing yelling. Two officers came downstairs with the lights in the hallway still off. When one of the officers and I were face to face, I scared him. So he pulls his gun, and all I know it's in the middle of my forehead. I threw my hands up. He asked me whom I was with, and I told him my little sister, please don't hurt her. He orders me to go upstairs and sit with my family. I see my father's frightened face and my little brother sitting on the couch. My dad tells me that

they won't let my mom cover up. I knew I had been hearing an argument. I looked in my parents' room, and one of the agents was yelling at her. Asking her if she had a gun under her pillow, is that why she wasn't getting up? Or if she was naked, then she needs to get up right now and get dressed and he's not leaving her side. He was pointing his gun and flashlight at her face. She kept arguing with him. All she wanted to do was cover herself. My father was handcuffed like a criminal.[6]

Curiously, this young woman's story sounded almost identical to that of another woman testifying, at the same forum, of a similar raid that took place in the same city, fifty years earlier. A Japanese-American woman, a former prisoner of war interned by the US government during World War II, told her harrowing account with fresh emotion:

My father was picked up by FBI agents and four Seattle policemen. It was the same day as my eldest sister's 11th birthday. In the early morning hours, the men pounded on the door, pushed aside my mother and invaded the house. They woke my father from his sleep, ordered him to dress and take care of his morning toiletries, all under strict observation by one of the officers. Meanwhile, agents searched throughout the house, ransacking closets, going through drawers and cupboards, only once giving an indication of what they were looking for. They did ask my sister if father owned "one of these" showing her his gun. To this day, she recalls her emphatic response of "No" as she watched in repulsed silence as one of the men sifted his hands through the sugar canister and rice container. When they left, taking my father with them, the house was in chaos. It was one of two times I ever saw my mother cry.[7]

The presentations were disturbing not just for the individual and collective experiences that they reflect, but because they had happened almost exactly fifty years apart and yet the stories were practically identical. Like many activists, I functioned under the assumption that as a collective human society, we were always, almost inevitably, improving. Progress was synonymous with the passage of time and those working for social change would have increased measures of success. But the stories of current victims of government repression, sounding almost identical to victims from decades past belied the idea that trajectory of change forever leaned towards progress and enlightenment.

"Repression," Serge comments, "can really only live off fear." But that is not the end of the matter as he goes on to ask: "But is fear enough to remove need, thirst for justice, intelligence, reason, idealism—all those revolutionary forces that express the formidable, profound impulse of the economic factors of a revolution? Relying on intimidation, the reactionaries forget that they will cause more indignation, more hatred, more thirst for martyrdom, than real fear. They only intimidate the weak; they exasperate the best forces and temper the resolution of the strongest."

After recent political setbacks, many people, hoping and working for serious change, had a "wake-up" call. Instead of decreasing, one after another, new tools of repression made their way into our daily lives. Activists began to look at the struggle with new appreciation for its length and breadth. The realization is dawning on many that this is not short-term resistance. In the words of a colleague, this is a marathon, not a sprint and we need to prepare for it. Serge was in it for the long haul, understanding the enduring demands of serious political reform. As many activists change their tactics and views of their work, Serge becomes ever more relevant. An intellectual and activist, he lived and thought optimistically. His friend Julian Gorkín called him an "eternal vagabond in search of the ideal." And in these days, as we are bound to suffer losses and falter, Serge has something timeless to teach and inspire us:

> Our mistakes were honorable. And even from a point of view less absurdly exalted, we were not so wrong. There is more falsification of ideas now than real confusion, and it is our own discoveries that are falsified. I feel humiliated only for the people who despair because we have been defeated. What is more natural and inevitable than to be beaten, to fail a hundred times, a thousand times, before succeeding? How many times does a child fall before he learns to walk? . . . The main thing is to have strong nerves, everything depends on that. And lucidity . . . Human destiny will brighten.[8]

Dalia Hashad
New York, 2005

chronology

1890

Victor Lvovich Kibalchich (Victor Serge) born on December 30 in Brussels to a family of Narodnik sympathizers who had fled from Russia after the assassination of Alexander II.

1908

Works as a photographer's apprentice and joins the socialist Jeunes-Gardes. Spends a short period in an anarchist "utopian" community in the Ardennes.

Leaves for Paris.

1910–11

Becomes editor of the French magazine *Anarchie.*

Implicated in the trial of the anarchists known as the Bonnot Gang. Despite arrest, he refuses to turn informer and is sentenced to five years' prison. Three of his codefendants are guillotined.

1917–18

Released from prison Serge is exiled from France. Goes to Barcelona where he participates in the syndicalist uprising.

Writes his first article as "Victor Serge." Leaves Barcelona to join the Russian army in France. Is detained for over a year in a French concentration camp as a Bolshevik suspect.

1919

Arrives in Petrograd at the height of the Civil War and starts work with Zinoviev organizing the Communist International (Comintern).

1920–22

Participates in Comintern congresses and edits various international journals.

Exposes czarist secret police archives.

1923–26

Represents the Comintern and is editor of *Imprekor* in Berlin and Vienna.

Returns to the Soviet Union to take part in the last stand of the Left Opposition against Stalin.

1927

Series of articles on the Chinese Revolution in which he criticizes Stalin's complacence towards the nationalist Kuomintang and draws attention to the importance of Mao Tsetung.

1928

Expelled from the Communist Party, he is relieved of all official functions.

1928–33

Takes up writing again and sends his manuscripts to France, since publication in the Soviet Union is impossible. Apart from many articles, he produces *Year One of the Russian Revolution* (1930); *Men in Prison* (1930); *Birth of Our Power* (1931) and *Conquered City* (1932).

1933

Arrested and deported to Orenburg in Central Asia, where he is joined by his young son, Vlady.

1935

Oppositionists raise the "Case of Victor Serge" at the Congress for the Defense of Culture in Paris where intellectuals campaign for his freedom.

1936

Released from Orenburg, Serge is deprived of Soviet citizenship. His manuscripts are confiscated and he is expelled from the USSR. He settles first in Brussels, then in Paris. His return to Europe is accompanied by a slander campaign in the Communist press.

1937

From Lenin to Stalin and *Destiny of a Revolution* are published. He is elected a councillor to the Spanish POUM (Independent Marxist Party) and campaigns against the Moscow trials.

1940

Leaves Paris just as the Nazis advance. In Marseilles, he struggles for months to obtain a visa. He finally finds refuge in Mexico.

1940-47

Lives in isolation and poverty in Mexico where he writes *The Case of Comrade Tulayev* and *Memoirs of a Revolutionary.*

1947

Victor Serge dies on November 17 and is buried as a "Spanish Republican" in the French section of the Mexico City cemetery.

author's preface to the 1925 French edition
Victor Serge

With the victory of the Russian Revolution, the whole mechanism of the most modern, most powerful, most battle-hardened political police, which had taken shape in over fifty years of bitter struggles against the leaderships of a great people, fell into the hands of the revolutionaries.

An acquaintance with the methods and proceedings of this police force is of immediate practical interest for every revolutionary, for the defense of capitalism everywhere uses the same tools; and moreover all police forces work together and are similar to each other.

The science of revolutionary struggle which the Russians acquired in over half a century of immense effort and sacrifice will have to be acquired in a much shorter space of time by revolutionaries in countries where action is developing today, in the circumstances created by the war, by the victory of the Russian proletariat and the defeats of the international proletariat—the crisis of world capitalism, the birth of the Communist International, the marked development of class consciousness among the bourgeoisie, with fascism, military dictatorship, White Terror and antiworking class laws; revolutionaries need this knowledge today. They will perhaps suffer fewer losses if given good warning of the means the enemy has at its disposal. There is thus good basis for practical reasons to study the main instrument of all reaction and all repression, that is, the apparatus for strangling all healthy revolt known as the police. The weapon perfected by the Russian autocracy to defend its existence — the Okhrana (Defensive), the general security police of the Russian Empire — has fallen into our hands enabling us this analysis.

To make the most thorough study would require leisure, which the author of these lines does not possess. The pages you are about to read do not make any claim to fulfill this task. They will, I hope, be adequate in giving comrades a warning and enabling them to see an important truth which struck me on my very first visit to the Russian police archives: there is no force in the world which can hold back the revolutionary tide when it rises, and that all police forces, however Machiavellian, scientific or criminal, are virtually impotent against it.

This work, published for the first time in the *Bulletin Communiste* in November 1921, has been carefully completed. The practical and theoretical questions, which a study of the workings of such a police force cannot fail to raise in the mind of a worker reading it, are examined in two new sections. Section "Simple advice to revolutionaries," which despite its obvious simplicity is very useful, outlines the fundamental rules of the workers' defense against surveillance, informing and provocation.

Since the war and the October Revolution, the working

class can no longer be content with carrying out solely negative and destructive tasks. The epoch of civil wars has begun. Whether they are posed today, or not for "some years," the many questions relating to the seizure of power still exist today for most communist parties. At the beginning of 1923, capitalist order in Europe might have appeared sufficiently stable to discourage the impatient. By the end of the year, however, the "peaceful" occupation of the Ruhr was to raise over Germany the powerfully real specter of revolution.

Now, all action aimed at the destruction of capitalist institutions needs to be complemented by the preparation, at least in theory, of the creative work of tomorrow. "The urge to destroy," Bakunin used to say, "is also the creative urge." This profound thought, which when taken literally has sent many revolutionaries astray, has just become practical reality. The same class struggle outlook today leads communists to destroy and create at the same time. Just as antimilitarism today needs to be complemented by the preparation of the Red Army, the problem of repression posed by the police and bourgeois justice has a positive side of great importance. It is necessary to define the main lines of it, to get to know the means the enemy has at his disposal and to get to know the full extent of our own tasks.

Victor Serge
March 1925

1 THE RUSSIAN OKHRANA

a special kind of policeman

The Okhrana took over in 1881 from the notorious Third Section of the Ministry of the Interior, fully developing after 1900, when a new generation of police was put in charge. The old officers of the constabulary, in particular the higher ranks, considered it contrary to military honor to occupy themselves with certain aspects of police business. The new school overrode such scruples, and undertook to organize the secret police on a scientific basis, carrying out provocation, informing and betrayal inside the revolutionary parties. It was to produce talented, erudite men like Colonel Spiridovich who left us a voluminous *History of the Socialist Revolutionary Party* and a *History of the Social Democratic Party.*

Special attention was given to the recruitment, education and professional training of officers of this police force. At Police Headquarters, a thoroughly documented file including many interesting details was kept on each person. Character, level of education, intelligence and service record were all noted down in an eminently practical spirit. One officer, for example, is described as "limited" — all right for secondary jobs and only requiring firm handling; while another, the file points out, is "inclined to pay court to the ladies."

Among the many questions on the form, the following are

particularly striking: "Does he have a good knowledge of the statutes and programs of any of the parties? Which parties?" We find that our friend who runs after the ladies "has a good knowledge of socialist-revolutionary and anarchist ideas, a passable knowledge of the Social Democratic Party and a superficial knowledge of the Polish Socialist Party." Note the careful grading of learning. A further examination of this file shows our policeman being asked whether he "followed courses in the history of the revolutionary movement?" "In which parties he had secret agents working? How many? Are they intellectuals, or workers?"

To train its experts, the Okhrana organized courses in which each party's origins, program, methods and even the life histories of its better-known members were studied.

It should be noted that this Russian police force, trained to do the most sensitive political police work, no longer had anything in common with the local constabularies of Western European countries. Its equivalent is to be found in the secret police of all capitalist states.

external surveillance— being followed

At the start, all surveillance is from the outside. This always involves following the individual, getting to know his activities, movements and contacts, and then finding out his plans. "Tailing" sections are developed by all police forces, and the Russian outfit clearly provides us with a prototype of all similar services.

In Russia, "tails," like "secret agents" — who in fact were spies and provocateurs — belonged to the Okhrana or Political Police. They were in the investigation service, which could only keep someone under arrest for a month. After that, the investigation service would generally hand its prisoners over to Police Headquarters, who would pursue inquiries.

External surveillance was the simplest of the services. Its many agents, whose identity photographs we now possess, were paid fifty rubles a month for one task: to spy on the person they were assigned to — hour after hour, day after day — with no interruption whatsoever. In principle, undoubtedly to pre-vent betrayal, or any blunders, they were not supposed to know the name of the person, or the aim of the espionage. The person under surveillance was given a nickname: Blondie, the Housekeeper, Vladimir, the Coachman, etc. We found these nicknames at the head of the daily reports, bound in thick volumes, in which the agents set out their observations. The reports are written in minute detail and without a gap. The text generally goes more or less like this:

> On April 17, at 9:54 a.m., the Housekeeper left home, posted two letters in the mailbox on the corner of Pushkin Street; went into various shops on Boulevard X; at 10:30 went into No. 13 Z Street, left at 11:20, etc.

In the most serious cases, two agents spied on the same person unbeknown to each other. Their reports were later cross-checked against the other.

These daily reports were sent to the police to be analyzed by specialists. These officers — the backroom boys — were dangerously perceptive. They would draw up tables showing a person's deeds and actions, the number of visits, their length and regularity, etc. Sometimes, these tables brought out the importance of one member's relationships and his or her probable influence.

The Police Chief Zubatov—who around 1905 tried to gain control of the workers' movement in the great centers, by setting up his own unions in them—brought this system of espionage to its highest level of perfection. His special brigades could follow a person throughout Russia, even throughout Europe, moving with him or her from one city to the next, or from one country to the next.

Secret agents did not go short on expenses. The expenditure sheet of one of them for the month of January 1905, gives us a figure for general expenses of 637.35 rubles. To get an idea of the kind of credit a mere informer like this enjoyed, it should be remembered that at this time a student could easily live on twenty-five rubles a month. Around 1911 it became customary to send foreign agents abroad to keep watch on émigrés and make contact with the European police. From then on His Imperial Majesty's informers were at home in every capital city in the world.

The Okhrana had the special mission of seeking out and placing under constant surveillance those revolutionaries considered the most dangerous, mainly terrorists, or members of the Socialist Revolutionary Party who practiced terrorism. Its agents always had to carry with them collections of fifty to seventy photographs—among which we can pick out Savinkov, the late Nathanson, Argunov, Avksentiev (alas!), Karelin, Ovsianikov, Vera Figner, Peshkova (Madame Gorki) and Fabrikant. They also carried copies of Marx's portrait, since the presence of such pictures in a room, or a book, was regarded to be significant.

External surveillance was used not only against the enemies of the *ancien régime*. We have in our possession records, which show that even the activities and movements of the ministers of the Empire did not escape the vigilance of the police. For example, "A Record of the Monitoring of Telephone Conversations" at the War Ministry in 1916, tells us how many times a day different members of the court asked after the precarious health of Madame Sukhomlinov!

the secrets of provocation

The most important section of the Russian police was unquestionably its "secret service," a polite name for the provocation agency, whose origins go back to the first revolutionary struggles, developing to an extraordinary degree after the 1905 revolution.

Only policemen (force officers) who had undergone special training, instruction and selection were engaged in the recruitment of agents provocateurs. The degree of their success in this field was taken into account when grading and promoting them. Precise instructions established the very finest details of the relationship between agents provocateurs and secret collaborators. Highly paid specialists collated all the information supplied by the provocateurs, studied it, sorted it out and cataloged it in reports.

At the Okhrana buildings (16 Fontanka, Petrograd), a secret room entered only by the chief of police and the officer in charge of sorting documents, was the center of the secret service. Its basic contents consisted of a filing system on the provocateurs, in which we found over thirty-five thousand names. In most cases, as a precaution, the name of the "secret agent" was replaced by a pseudonym. After the triumph of the revolution, when these reports fell in their entirety into the comrades' hands, the identification of many of these wretches proved particularly difficult.

The name of the provocateur was to be known to no one but the head of the Okhrana and the officer responsible for maintaining permanent contact with him. Generally, only pseudonyms were used, even when the provocateurs signed the monthly receipts for their salaries, which were paid as normally and regularly as to other state employees for sums ranging from three, 10 or 15 rubles a month up to a maximum of 150 or 200. The administration however, distrustful of its agents and anxious that police officers should not invent imaginary collaborators, often carried out detailed investigations into different branches of their organization. A fully authorized inspector personally checked up on secret collaborators, interviewed them at his discretion, and either sacked them, or gave them a rise. We should add that reports from such inspectors were, as far as possible, carefullly checked out against each other.

directive on the recruitment and operation of agents provocateurs

Another document, which can be considered as the A.B.C. of provocation, is the *Directive on the Secret Service* — a twenty-seven page, duplicated, small-format booklet. Our copy (numbered 35) also carries in the upper corners the following three warnings: "Highly secret," "Confidential use," "Professional secret." What an insistence on mystery! The reader will soon see why.

This document, which reveals a good knowledge of psychology, practical questions, a remarkably farsighted intelligence and a very odd mixture of cynicism and official moral hypocrisy, will one day be of interest to psychologists.

It begins with some general guidelines:

> The Political Police must prepare to destroy the revolutionary centers at the moment their activity is greatest and not allow their work to be diverted by dwelling on secondary undertakings.

So the principle is: let the movement develop, the better to liquidate it later on.

> Secret agents must be paid at a fixed rate, proportional to services rendered.

The police must:

> take the greatest care not to give away their collaborators. To this end, do not arrest, or free them except when other members of equal importance belonging to the same revolutionary organizations may be arrested, or freed.

The police must:

> help their collaborators gain the confidence of the revolutionaries.

There follows a chapter on recruitment.

> The recruitment of secret agents is the constant preoccupation of the head of investigation and his collaborators. They must let slip no opportunity of procuring agents, even when it does not seem very hopeful . . .
>
> This is an extremely delicate task. Carrying it out involves making contact with political prisoners . . .

The following must be considered suitable to enter the service:

> Revolutionaries of weak character, those disillusioned with, or aggrieved by the party, those living in poverty, those who have escaped from places of exile, or are under sentence of exile . . .

The directive recommends a "careful" study of their weaknesses and how to exploit those weaknesses. For example, engage in conversation with their friends and relatives and "constantly increase contacts with workers, witnesses, relatives, etc., without ever losing sight of the objective . . ."

Extraordinary duplicity of the human mind! I give here a literal translation of three disconcerting lines:

> We can make use of revolutionaries living in poverty who, without renouncing their convictions, agree out of necessity to hand over information . . .

Were there then such people? But let us continue:

> Placing informers among prisoners is extremely useful.

When a person appears ready to enter the service — when, for example, in addition to knowing a revolutionary to be embittered, in material difficulties, or perhaps disoriented by his own errors — there are also sufficient grounds for charges to get a hold over him:

> Capture the whole group to which he belongs and bring the person in question before the Chief of Police; have serious reasons for charging him, while reserving the possibility of freeing him at the same time as other jailed revolutionaries, so as not to cause suspicion.
>
> Interrogate the person individually. To convince him, make use of the quarrels between groups, the mistakes of members, things which have wounded his self-esteem.

Reading these lines, one gets a glimpse of the paternal policeman taking pity on his victim: "Of course, while you go off to do forced labor for your ideas, your Comrade X, who has given you such a bad time, will be doing all right at your expense. What do you expect? The good pay the price for the sinners!"

This may have an effect on a weak person, or someone driven crazy by the years of exile hanging over him.

> So far as possible, have several collaborators in each organization. The service must direct its collaborators, not be directed by them. Secret agents must never know the information given by their colleagues.

And here is a passage Machiavelli would not have been ashamed of:

> A collaborator working in secondary posts in a revolutionary organization can be promoted within it by means of the arrest of more important members.

Keeping provocation an absolute secret is of course one of the main concerns of the police:

> The agent swears to keep his work an absolute secret. Hence, on entering the service he should not in the least modify his usual habits.

There are strict guidelines for communication with precautions, which would be difficult to improve upon:

> Meetings may be assigned only to highly trustworthy colleagues. They will take place in clandestine apartments, consisting of various rooms with no direct communication between them, where, should it be necessary, different visitors can be isolated from each other. The tenant must be in public employment. He will never be able to receive private visits, nor will he be able to get to know the secret agents, or speak to them. He will be obliged to open the door to them in person and check before they go out that there is no one on the stairs. Interviews will take place in locked rooms. No papers must be left lying about. Care must be taken not to seat any visitor near windows, or mirrors. At the least suspicious sign, move apartments. [The provocateur] can under no circumstances present himself at Police Headquarters. He can undertake no important mission without the agreement of his chief.

Meetings were fixed by means of prearranged signs.

Correspondence was sent to agreed addresses:

> Letters from secret collaborators must be written in unrec-
> ognizable writing and should only contain ordinary expressions.
> Use paper and envelopes in keeping with the social standing
> of the addressee. Write in invisible ink. The collaborator sends
> his letters himself. When receiving them, he is obliged to burn
> them as soon as they are read. The addresses used should never
> be written down.

One serious problem was how to free a secret agent arrested
with those he had betrayed. The directive does not advise
resorting to escape in such cases, since:

> Escape attracts the attention of the revolutionaries. Before the
> liquidation of any organization, consult the secret agents about
> which people to leave at liberty, so as not to give away our
> sources of information.

a monograph of provocation in Moscow (1912)

Another item chosen from the archives of provocation gives
us a clear picture of the extent it had reached. The document in question is a kind of monograph on provocation in
Moscow in 1912. It is the report of a high-ranking official,
Mr. Vissarianov, commissioned that year to carry out an
inspection of Moscow's secret service.

Mr. Vissarianov carried out his mission from April 1 to
April 22. His report forms a thick duplicated booklet. Every
provocateur—listed under a pseudonym of course—is the

subject of a detailed note, some of which are very curious.

On April 6, 1912, there were in Moscow 55 official agents provocateurs, distributed as follows:

Socialist Revolutionaries, 17; Social Democrats, 20; anarchists, three; students (schools' movement), 11; philanthropic institutions, etc., two; scientific societies, one; zemstvos [district and provincial assemblies], one. Furthermore, "the secret service in Moscow also keeps watch on the press, the Octobrists (Cadets, or Constitutional Democratic Party), Burtzev's agents, the Armenians, the extreme right and the Jesuits."

The collaborators were described in fairly concise reports:

> Social Democratic Party, Bolshevik faction. "Portnoi" ("the Tailor"), a wood turner, intelligent. In the service since 1910. Gets 100 rubles a month. Very well informed collaborator. Will be candidate to the Duma. Took part in the Prague Bolshevik conference. Out of five revolutionaries sent from Russia to this conference, three were arrested.

On the question of the Bolsheviks' Prague conference, our high-ranking officer further congratulates himself on the results obtained by the secret agents. Some were able to infiltrate the Central Committee, and one of them, an informer, was commissioned by the party to smuggle literature into Russia. "This way we have the whole propaganda supply in our hands," our policeman affirms.

A digression is in order here. Yes, at this point they did have the Bolshevik propaganda supply in their hands. But was the effect of this propaganda any less? Did Lenin's written words lose any of their value for passing through the wretched hands of informers? The strength of the revolutionary message lies within it, it has only to be heard. It doesn't matter who transmits it. The success of the Okhrana would really have been decisive if it had been able to prevent the Bolshevik organizations being supplied with literature from abroad. But it was only able to do so to a certain extent, at the risk of exposing its forces.

files on agents provocateurs

What is an agent provocateur? We have thousands of files which give abundant documentation on these wretched people and their activities. Let's cast an eye over a few of them:

File 378. Julia Orestovna Serova (alias "Pravdivy" — "the Truthteller" — and "Ulyanova"). When the minister raised a question about the service record of this provocateur, sacked because her cover had been blown, the Chief of Police replied by enumerating her first-rate achievements. The letter consists of four long pages. I shall summarize it, quoting almost literally:

> Julia Orestovna Serova was employed from September 1907 to 1910 in surveillance of the social-democratic organizations. Occupying relatively important positions in the party, she was thereby able to render great services, both in Petrograd and in the provinces. A whole series of arrests was brought about thanks to information from her.
>
> In September 1907, with her help, the Duma Deputy Sergei Saltykov was arrested.
>
> At the end of April 1908 another four members were arrested: Rykov, Nogin, "Gregorii" and "Kamenev."

On May 9, 1908, an entire party meeting was arrested due to her information.

In the autumn of 1908, the Central Committee member, "Innocent" Dubrovsky, was arrested.

In February 1909 she had the equipment for a clandestine printing press seized and the party's passports office raided.

On March 1, 1909, she had the whole of the Saint Petersburg Committee arrested.

She also assisted in the arrest of a group of expropriators (May 1907), had consignments of literature seized, and in particular had blocked the transportation of illegal literature through Vilna. In 1908 she kept us informed of all the meetings of the Central Committee, and also informed us of its composition. In 1909 she took part in a conference of the party abroad, reporting on it, and kept watch on the activities of Alexei Rykov.

Such was her fine service record.

But Serova's cover was blown in the end. Her husband, a deputy in the Duma, announced in the daily press of the capital that he no longer considered her to be his wife. His meaning was understood. As she could no longer be of service, her superiors in the hierarchy bid her farewell. She fell into poverty. Her file is crammed with her letters to the head of the Political Police: protestations of loyalty, reminders of services rendered, requests for help.

I have read nothing more miserable than these letters, written in the nervous, hurried handwriting of a female intellectual. The "retired provocateur," as she calls herself at one point, appears to be at bay, tormented by poverty, in total moral disarray. How was she to live? Serova was useless with her hands. Her state of anxiety prevented her from finding a solution — a simple, reasonable job.

On August 16, 1912, she wrote to the Chief of Police:

> My two children, the elder of whom is five years old, have no clothes or shoes. I have no furniture left. I am too poorly dressed to find work. If you do not grant me assistance, I shall be forced to commit suicide.

They sent her 150 rubles.

On September 17, in another letter, enclosing a letter for her husband which the Chief of Police was to be sure to post, she said:

> You will see, in the last letter I am writing to my husband, that on the point of putting an end to my life I am still denying having worked for the police. I have decided to put an end to it all. I am neither joking nor trying to attract attention. I no longer believe it is possible for me to begin a new life.

But Serova was not to kill herself. A few days later she was denouncing an old gentleman for concealing arms.

The letters finally amounted to a thick volume. Here is a moving one — a few lines saying farewell to the man who had been her husband:

> I have often been bad to you. I had not even written to you until now. But forget all that was bad and remember only our life in common, our work in common and forgive me. I bid farewell to life. I am tired. I feel that too many things have broken inside me. Far be it from me to curse anyone; but curse the "comrades" all the same!

Where does sincerity begin in these letters and where does duplicity end? We do not know. We have before us a complex, painful, blemished, prostituted, naked soul.

Nonetheless, the police were not deaf to her entreaties. Each of Serova's letters, bearing handwritten comments from the head of the service, has the director's solution noted on it: "Send her 250 rubles," "Pay out fifty rubles." The ex-collaborator announces the death of one of her children. "Check it out," writes the director. Later, she asked them to supply her with a typewriter so that she could learn to type.

The police force had none to spare. Towards the end, the letters became more pressing:

> In the name of my children [she wrote on December 14] I write to you with tears and blood: grant me one last sum of 300 rubles. I will make do with that.

This was agreed, on condition that she left Petrograd. In all, in 1911, Serova received 743 rubles in three payments and next year, in 1912, six payments totaling 788 rubles. It was a considerable sum for the times.

After a final payment made in February 1914, Serova found a modest job with the railway administration. She soon lost it for pilfering small sums of money from her workmates. A note in the file says: "Guilty of extortion. No longer worthy of any confidence." Nonetheless, under the name of Petrova, she managed to get into the service of the railway police who found her out and sacked her. In 1915 she again sought the job of an informer. On January 28, 1917, on the eve of the revolution, this former secretary of a revolutionary committee wrote to "His Excellency, the Chief of Police," reminding him of her good and faithful service and proposing to keep him informed of the activity of the Social Democratic Party, which she could get her second husband to join:

> On the eve of the great events one feels to be coming, I suffer at being unable to help you . . .

File 383. "Osipov" — Nicolai Nicolayevich Veretsky, the son of a priest. A student. A secret collaborator from 1903, informing on the Social Democratic organization and the school youth of Pavlograd.

Sent to Saint Petersburg by the party in 1905, his mission being to smuggle arms into Finland, he presented himself immediately at Police Headquarters to receive instructions.

When his comrades became suspicious, he was arrested, spending three months in the secret section of the Okhrana. On release he was sent abroad "in order to rehabilitate himself in the eyes of the revolutionaries."

I quote verbatim from the conclusion of one report:

> Veretsky gives the impression of being a very intelligent and cultured young man, very modest, conscientious and honest; it has to be said in his favor that he gives the greater part of his salary of 150 rubles to his aged parents.

In 1915 this excellent youth withdrew from the service still receiving a further twelve monthly payments of seventy-five rubles each.

File 317. "The Invalid": Vladimir Ivanovich Lorberg. A worker. Writes clumsily. Works in a factory and gets ten rubles a month.

A proletarian provocateur.

File 81. Sergei Vasilievich Praotsev, son of a member of Narodnaya Volya (People's Will), boasts of having grown up in a revolutionary environment and of having extensive, useful connections.

There are thousands of similar files in our possession. The lowness and wretchedness of some human beings is unfathomable.

We have not yet had access to the files of the secret collaborators whose names are given below. They should, nonetheless, be mentioned here as being characteristic cases: one an able intellectual, the other a popular leader.

Stanislaw Brzozowski, a Polish writer of considerable talent, looked up to by the youth, and the author of critical essays on Kant, Zola, Mikhailovsky and Avenarius—"the herald of socialism, in which he saw the most profound synthesis of the human spirit, and which he wanted to make into a philosophical system embracing nature and society" (*Naprzod*, May 5, 1908)—and author of the revolutionary novel, *The Flame*. For his report on revolutionary and "progressive" circles, he drew 150 rubles a month from the Okhrana in Warsaw. The life and soul of the workers' movement in Saint Petersburg and Moscow before the 1905 revolution, Father Gapon, was the organizer of the workers' demonstration of January 1905. The crowd of petitioners, led by two priests carrying a portrait of the czar, was drenched in blood under the windows of the Winter Palace by volleys of rifle fire. Father Gapon, the very incarnation of one moment in the Russian Revolution, ended up selling himself to the Okhrana. Convicted of the crime of provocation, he was executed by the Socialist Revolutionary, Ruthenberg.

a ghost from the past

Even today we are far from having identified all the Okhrana agents provocateurs whose files we now have.

Not a month passes without the Revolutionary Tribunals of the Soviet Union passing judgment on some of these men. They are met and identified by chance. In 1924, one such wretch appeared, coming back to us from a fifty-year past as though with a sudden rush of nausea — a real ghost. This specter called to mind a page of history, which we insert here simply to cast into these sordid pages a little of the light of revolutionary heroism.

This agent provocateur gave thirty-seven years' good service (from 1880 to 1917) and, even as an old man, was wily enough to give the Cheka the slip for seven whole years.

Around 1879, the twenty-year-old student Okladsky, a revol-utionary from the age of fifteen, a member of the Narodnaya Volya Party and a terrorist, planned together with Zheliabov, an attempt on the life of Czar Alexander II. They were going to blow up the imperial train. It passed over the mines without incident. The infernal machine did not work. An accident? So it was thought at the time, but sixteen revolutionaries, including Okladsky, had to answer for this "crime." Okladsky was condemned to death. Was this the beginning of his brilliant career, or had it already begun? A pardon from the emperor commuted his sentence to life imprisonment.

It was, in any case, the beginning of the series of inesti-mable services Okladsky was to render to the czarist police. In the long list of revolutionaries he was to hand over, were four names which are among the finest in our history: Barannikov, Zheliabov, Trigoni and Vera Figner. Of these four, only Vera Nicolaevna Figner survived. She spent twenty years in the Schlüsselberg fortress. Barannikov died there. Trigoni, after suffering twenty years in Schlüsselberg and four in exile in Sakhalin, lived just long enough to see the overthrow of the autocracy before his death in June 1917. Zheliabov died on the gallows.

These brave figures were leaders of Narodnaya Volya, the first Russian revolutionary party, which, before the birth of the proletarian movement, had declared war on the autocracy. Their program was for a liberal revolution, which, if achieved, would have been an enormous step forward for Russia. In a period in which no other action was possible, they employed terrorism, constantly striking at the head of czarism, sometimes driving it mad and on March 1, 1881, beheading it. In the struggle of this handful of heroes against the powerfully armed old society, were forged the customs, traditions and outlook which, carried forward by the proletariat, were to temper many generations for the victory of October 1917.

Of all these heroes, perhaps the greatest was Alexander Zheliabov, who certainly rendered the greatest services to the party he had helped to found. Denounced by Okladsky, he was arrested on February 27, 1881, in an apartment on the Nevsky Prospekt, in the company of a young lawyer from Odessa, Trigoni, also a member of the mysterious Executive Committee of Narodnaya Volya. Two days later, the party's bombs blew Alexander II to pieces in a Saint Petersburg street. The following day, the legal authorities received an astounding letter from Zheliabov, written from the Peter and Paul Prison. Rarely has a judiciary and a monarchy met with such defiance. Rarely has the leader of a party carried out his last duty with such pride. The letter said:

> If the new sovereign, who receives his scepter from the hands of the revolution, plans to give the regicides the same punishment as of old; if he plans to execute Ryssakov, it would be a crying injustice to spare my life, since I have made so many attempts on the life of Alexander II, and only chance prevented my participation in his execution. I am very concerned that the government may be putting a higher price on formal justice than on real justice, and adorning the crown of the new monarch with the corpse of a young hero, solely for lack of formal proof against myself, a veteran of the revolution.
>
> With all my heart I protest against this iniquity. Only cowardice on the part of the government could explain why two gallows should not be raised instead of one.

The new czar, Alexander III, had in fact put up six gibbets for the regicides. At the last moment, a young pregnant woman, Jessy Helfman, was pardoned. Zheliabov died alongside his companion, Sophia Perovskaya, Ryssakov (who had turned traitor, to no avail), Mikhailov and the chemist Kibalchich. Mikhailov had to suffer being hanged three times. Twice, the hangman's rope broke. Twice, Mikhailov fell, wrapped in his shroud and hood, and stood up again of his own accord . . .

Meanwhile, the provocateur Okladsky, carried on with his services. Among the openhearted youth who tirelessly "went to the people," to poverty, prison, exile and death to open the way for revolution, it was easy enough to deal hidden blows! Scarcely had Okladsky arrived in Kiev, when he handed over Vera Nikolaevna Figner to the Police Chief

Sudekin. He worked in Tbilisi as a professional traitor, becoming an expert in the art of forming relationships with the best men there, gaining their friendship and feigning to share their enthusiasm, in order to one day point the finger and have his comrades buried alive . . . He receive the expected gratuity.

In 1889, the imperial police called him to Saint Petersburg. Minister Durnovo, absolving Okladsky of anything unworthy in his past, turned him into the "Honorable Citizen" Petrovsky; still of course a revolutionary and the confidant of revolutionaries. He was to remain on "active service" until the revolution of March 1917. Up until 1924 he managed to pass himself off as a peaceful inhabitant of Petrograd. Later, locked up in Leningrad in the very prison where many of his victims had awaited their death, he agreed to write a confession of his life up until the year 1890.

Beyond that date, the old agent provocateur refused to say a word. He spoke only about a past from which scarcely any of the revolutionaries survived, but which he had peopled with martyrs and with dead . . .

The Revolutionary Tribunal of Leningrad passed judgment on Okladsky in the first fortnight of January 1925. The revolution is not vengeful. This was a ghost from too remote a past, a past which was dead and buried. The trial, conducted by veterans of the revolution, seemed like a scientific debate on history and psychology. It was a study of the most pitiful of human documents. Okladsky was sentenced to ten years' imprisonment.

the case of Malinovsky

Let us dwell briefly on a case of provocation of which there are several examples in the history of the Russian revolutionary movement: provocation on the part of a party leader. Enter the enigmatic figure of Malinovsky.

One morning in 1918—the terrible year which followed the October Revolution, with civil war, requisitioning in the countryside, sabotage by technicians, conspiracies, the Czech uprising, foreign intervention, the infamous peace (as Lenin called it) of Brest-Litovsk, two assassination attempts on Vladimir Ilyich himself—one morning in that year, a man quite calmly appeared before the commandant of the Smolny Institute in Petrograd and said to him:

"I am the provocateur Malinovsky. I ask you to arrest me."

Humor has a place in all tragedy. Unmoved, the Smolny commandant nearly showed his untimely visitor the door.

"I have no orders to deal with this! And it's not my job to arrest you!"

"Then take me to the party committee!"

At the committee offices, he was recognized, with astonishment, as the most execrable, the most contemptible figure in the party. He was arrested.

His career, in brief, was as follows:

The good side: a difficult adolescence, three convictions for thieving. Very gifted, very active, a member of several organizations, so highly thought of that in 1910 he was asked to accept nomination to the Central Committee of the Russian Social Democratic Labor Party, and was elected to it at the Prague Bolshevik conference (1912). By the end of that year he was a Bolshevik deputy in the Fourth Imperial Duma. In 1913 he became president of the Bolshevik parliamentary faction.

The bad side: Okhrana informer (known as "Ernest," and later "the Tailor") from 1907. From 1910, he was on one hundred rubles a month (a princely rate). The ex-Chief of Police, Beletsky, says: "Malinovsky was the pride of the service, which was grooming him to be one of the leaders of the party." He had groups of Bolsheviks arrested in Moscow, Tula, etc.; he handed Milyutin, Nogin, Maria Smidovich, Stalin and Sverdlov over to the police. He handed over secret party ar-chives to the Okhrana. With the discreet but effective help of the police he was even elected to the Duma.

Once exposed, Malinovsky received hefty compensation from the Ministry of the Interior and disappeared. The war intervened. Taken prisoner in the fighting, he again became an active member in the concentration camps. Finally he returned to Russia, proclaiming to the Revolutionary Tribunal: "Have me shot!" He claimed to have suffered enormously from his dual existence; to have only really understood the revolution too late; and to have let himself be drawn on by ambition and the spirit of adventure. Krylenko mercilessly refuted this argument, sincere though it may have been: "The adventurer is playing his last card!" he said.

A revolution cannot halt to decipher psychological enigmas. Nor can it run the risk of being deceived once again by a turbulent, impassioned actor. The Revolutionary Tribunal delivered the verdict demanded by both the accuser and the accused. A few hours later that same night, Malinovsky was crossing an isolated courtyard in the Kremlin when he suddenly received a bullet in the back of the neck.

the mentality of the provocateur

This brings us to the question of the psychology of the provocateur. It is certainly a morbid psychology, but that should not surprise us unduly. We have seen, in the Okhrana's directive, what kind of people the police "work on" and what methods they use. Someone like Serova, considered a weak character, living in poverty, who works courageously as a party member. She is arrested. Abruptly torn out of her normal existence, she feels lost. Forced labor awaits her, perhaps the gallows; or she could say a word, just one word, about someone who actually had done her some wrong . . . She hesitates. An instant of cowardice is enough; and there is plenty of cowardice in the depths of a human being. The most terrible thing is that from now on, she will no longer be able to turn back . . . They have her now. If she refuses to go on, they will throw her first betrayal in her face in open court. As time passes she will become accustomed to the material advantages of this odious situation, all the

more because she will feel perfectly secure that her activity
is a secret . . .

There are however, not only people who are agents out
of cowardice. There are, much more dangerously, those
dilettantes and adventurers who believe in nothing, indif-
ferent to the ideal they have been serving, taken by the idea of
danger, intrigue, conspiracy — a complicated game in which
they can make fools of everyone. They may have talent,
their role may be almost undetectable. Malinovsky appears
to have been such a person. The Russian literature of the
period following the defeat of 1905 offers us several similarly
perverted psychological cases. The illegal revolutionary —
above all the terrorist — acquires a terrible cast of mind, a
formidable will, daring, love of danger . . . If then, following
a common shift of mentality, under the influence of petty
personal experiences — failures, disillusionment, intellectual
deviations — or of temporary defeats of the movement, it
turns out he loses his idealism, what is to become of him? If he
really is strong, he will steer clear of neuroticism and suicide;
but in some cases he may become a faithless adventurer, to
whom any means seem good to attain his personal ends.
And provocation is one means which they will certainly try
to put to him.

All mass movements involving thousands and thousands
of people experience similar murky episodes. This should not
surprise us. The action of such parasites has very little power
against the vigor and moral strength of the proletariat.

We believe that the more proletarian the revolutionary
movement, the more clearly and energetically communist
it is, the less danger will it face from agents provocateurs.

They will probably exist as long as the class battle goes on. But they are individuals to whom the habit of collective thought and work, strict discipline and action calculated by the masses and inspired by a scientific theory of the social situation, give the least chance of success. There is nothing more opposed to adventurism on a large or small scale, than the broad-based, serious, profound, methodical action of a great Marxist revolutionary party, even in illegality. Communist illegality is not the same as that of the *carbonari*. Communists do not prepare the insurrection in the same way as the Blanquists. The *carbonari* and the Blanquists were small groups of conspirators, led by a few intelligent, energetic idealists. A communist party, even if it is weak in numbers, always, by virtue of its ideology, represents the proletarian class. It incarnates the class-consciousness of hundreds of thousands, or millions of people. Its role is immense, since it is the role of the brain and of the whole nervous system, albeit inseparable from the aspirations, needs and activity of the whole proletariat—so that within it the designs of individuals, when they are not in line with the needs of the party (that is, of the proletariat[1]), lose much of their importance.

In this sense, the communist party is, among all the revolutionary organizations history has produced up to now, the least vulnerable to the blows of provocation.

provocation—
a two-edged sword

Certain special files contain offers of service addressed to the police. I have looked at random through a tome of foreign correspondence, in which there appear successively "a Danish subject possessing higher education" and "a Corsican student of good family" asking for employment in the secret police of His Majesty the Czar of Russia . . .

The repeated grants of financial aid to Serova bear witness to the great attention paid by the police to those who served them, even when no longer active. The administration only blacklisted agents caught in flagrante delicto committing fraud, or extortion. Described as "blackmailers" and black-listed, they lost all right to recognition from the state.

The others, however, could get anything they wanted: postponement, or exemption from military service, pardons, amnesties, different favors after being officially sentenced; temporary pensions, or travel grants—everything, even favors from the czar himself. The czar was even known to give long-standing provocateurs new first names and patronymics. According to orthodox doctrine the family name and patronymic had religious value. Therefore, the spiritual head of the Russian church was breaking the rules of his own religion. But nothing is too much for a good informer!

Provocation in the end became a real institution. The final count of those who, in the course of twenty years, had been in the revolutionary movement, and had been of service to the police, may vary between thirty-five thousand and forty thousand. It is estimated that about half of them were exposed.

A few thousand former provocateurs and informers still survive today within Russia, as it has not yet been possible to identify them all. Among this multitude there were individuals of daring, and even some who played an important role in the revolutionary movement.

At the head of the Socialist Revolutionary Party and its combat organization, up to 1909, was the engineer Evno Azev, who from 1890 onwards had been sending reports to the police signed with his own name. Azev was one of the organizers of the executions of Grand Duke Sergei, Minister Plehve and many others. It was he who first directed the work of such heroes as Kaliaev and Igor Sazonov,[2] then sent them to their death.

On the Bolshevik Central Committee, and leading its Duma faction, as we have seen, was the secret agent Malinovsky.

Provocation, when it becomes so widely extended, becomes a danger even to the regime it serves, and above all to those at the head of this regime. It is known, for example, that one of the highest officials of the Ministry of the Interior, the policeman Rachkovsky, knew and approved of the plans for the execution of Plehve and of Grand Duke Sergei. Stolypin,[3] well informed on this score, was accompanied whenever he went out by the Police Chief Gerasimov, whose presence he took to be a guarantee against attacks instigated by provocateurs. Stolypin was nonetheless killed by the anarchist Bagrof, who had belonged to the police.

Provocation, in spite of everything, was still flourishing at the moment the revolution broke out. The agents provocateurs received their last month's salary in the last few days of February 1917, a week before the overthrow of the autocracy.

Committed revolutionaries found themselves tempted to take advantage of provocation. Petrov, the Socialist Revolutionary, who has left us intensely tragic memoirs, entered the Okhrana the better to fight it. Imprisoned, after meeting with an initial refusal from the Chief of Police, he pretended to be mad in order to be sent to a place of exile from which he could escape, did so, and returned as a free man to offer his services. But, soon convinced that he had gone too far, and that in spite of himself he was betraying, Petrov committed suicide after executing Colonel Karpov (1909).

The Maximalist[4] Solomon Ryss (Mortimer), the organizer of an extremely daring terrorist group (1906–07), managed for a time to hoodwink the Service, of which he had become a secret collaborator. The case of Solomon Ryss[5] is a notable, almost unbelievable exception, which can only be explained by the particular habits of the Okhrana and its general disarray after the 1905 revolution. As a general rule, it is impossible to hoodwink the police; impossible for a revolutionary to penetrate its secrets. The most trusted secret agent only has contact with one or two policemen, whom he can get nothing out of; but to whom the least word is of use, even the lies they are told, which are soon brought to light.

The development of provocation, however, often led the Okhrana to set up complicated intrigues in which they did not always have the last word. So, in 1907, it became necessary for their plans for Ryss himself to escape. To achieve this, the police chief himself did not draw the line at crime. Following his instructions, two police officers organized the revolutionary's escape. Through bad management, the judicial inquiry revealed their part in the affair. Court-martialed and officially stripped of rank by their superiors, they were sentenced to forced labor.

russian informers abroad

The ramifications of the Okhrana of course extended abroad. Their archives contained information on the large number of people then living beyond the frontiers of the Empire, including some who had never been in Russia at all. Although I only came to Russia for the first time in 1919, I found a series of files on myself. The Russian police followed the activities of revolutionaries abroad with the greatest attention. On the case of the Russian anarchists Troianovsky and Kirichek, caught in Paris during the war, I found voluminous files in Petrograd. They included the complete report of the inquiry held in the Paris Palace of Justice. For the rest, be they Russians or foreigners, the anarchists were everywhere kept under special surveillance by the Okhrana, which for that purpose maintained a constant correspondence with the security services of London, Rome, Berlin, etc.

In every major capital city there was a Russian police chief in permanent residence. During the war, Krassilnikov, officially an adviser at the embassy, occupied this delicate position.

At the time the Russian Revolution broke out, some fifteen agents provocateurs were operating in Paris in the different

Russian émigré groups. When the last ambassador of the last czar had to hand over the legation to a successor appointed by the Provisional Government, a commission consisting of highly regarded members of the émigré colony in Paris undertook a study of Krassilnikov's papers. They identified the secret agents without difficulty. Among other surprises, they found that a member of the French press, who had always appeared to be a good patriot, had been around the Rue de Grenelle as an informer and spy. He was Monsieur Raymond Recouly, then a journalist on *Le Figaro*, where he was in charge of the foreign desk. In his secret collaboration with Krassilnikov, Recouly, following the rule for informers, had changed his name to the not very literary pseudonym of "Rat Catcher." A dog's name for a dog's job. The "Rat Catcher" reported to the Okhrana on his colleagues in the French press. He put forward Okhrana policy in *Le Figaro* and elsewhere. He was paid five hundred francs a month. His activities are notorious.

They can be read about complete, in printed form; they were apparently published in Paris in 1918 in a voluminous report by Agafanov, a member of the Paris Émigrés' Commission of Inquiry into Russian provocateurs in France. The members of this commission—some of whom must still be living in Paris—will certainly not have forgotten the "Rat Catcher" Recouly. René Marchand, meanwhile, in 1924, published in *L'Humanité* proof, taken from the Okhrana's Petrograd archives, of M. Recouly's police activity. This gentleman did no more than issue a denial which no one believed, yet he was not rejected by his colleagues.[6] And for good reason. Given the extent of the corruption of the press by foreign governments, his case was not very remarkable.

mail-opening
and the international police

Krassilnikov also had under his orders a whole team of detectives, informers, and various unspecified office workers employed on lowly jobs, such as reading the correspondence of revolutionaries (special censorship office, etc.).

In 1913–14 (and I don't think it changed in any important respect up until the revolution) the secret agency of the Okhrana in France was in practice directed by a certain Bittard-Monin, who received one thousand francs a month. From the receipts for fees signed by his agents I have taken a list of their names and places of residence, as follows:

Secret agents abroad placed under the direction of Bittard-Monin (Paris): E. Invernitzi (Calvi, Corsica), Henri Durin (Genoa), Sambaine (Paris), A. or R. Sauvard (Cannes), Vogt (Menton), Berthold (Paris), Fontaine (Cap Martin), Henri Neuhaus (Cap Martin), Vincent Vizardelli (Grenoble), Barthes (San Remo), Charles Delangle (San Remo), Georges Coussonet (Cap Martin), O. Rougeaux (Menton), E. Levêque (Cap Martin), Fontana (Cap Martin), Artur Frumtento (Alassis). Sustrov or Surkhanov and David (Paris), Dussossois (Cap Martin), R. Gottlieb (Nice), Godard (Nice), Roselli (Zurich), Mme. G Richard (Paris), Jean Abersold (London), J. Bint (Cannes), Karl Voltz (Berlin), Mlle. Drouchot, Mme. Tiercelin, Mme. Fagon, Jollivet, Rivet.

Three people had a pension from the Russian agency in Paris: Widow Farse (or Farce?), Widow Rigo (or Rigault?) and N.N. Shashnikov.

The temporary presence of several agents in Cap Martin,

or other less important places is due to the need to keep them out of the way. None of these agents found it inconvenient to move for a while.

They had managed to organize a marvelous system of interception throughout Europe. In Petrograd we have bundles of copies of letters exchanged between Paris and Nice, Rome and Geneva, Berlin and London, etc. All of Savinkov's and Chernov's correspondence at the time both were living in France has been preserved in the police archives in Petrograd. Correspondence between Haase and Dan[7] was also intercepted, together with that of many others. How? The concierge, or mailman of the addressee, or simply a post office employee—who doubtless received generous remuneration—held onto letters addressed to the person under surveillance for a few hours only—the time needed to copy them. The copies were often made by people who did not know the language used by the writers of the letters: otherwise insignificant mistakes give this away. They also copied the seal and the address, and the copy was sent to Petrograd at top speed.

Naturally, the Russian police abroad collaborated with the local police forces.[8] While the agents provocateurs, unbeknown to all, carried on in their role of revolutionaries, Krassilnikov's detectives were working around them, officially unknown but in effect harbored and assisted. Little characteristic details show what kind of help they were getting from the French authorities. The agent Francesco Leone, who had been in contact with Burtzev,[9] had agreed to hand over, for money, some of Bittard-Monin's secrets. His colleague, Fontana, whose photograph he had stolen, wounded him with a blow from his cane in a café near the

Gare de Lyon (Paris, June 28, 1913). When the aggressor was arrested and a revolver and two French security police identification cards were found on him, he was sent to the police station on the quadruple charge of "usurping official functions, carrying forbidden arms, wounding and threatening to kill." Twenty-four hours later he was freed by the intervention of Krassilnikov — after an official denial that he was a Russian police agent. As for the indiscreet Leone, the Russian embassy got him expelled from France. A letter from Krassilnikov[10] informed the head of security of all these incidents and kept him in touch with the moves in hand to get Burtzev deported from Italy.

In another letter, the same Krassilnikov informs the Okhrana that a parliamentary question from the socialists on the operations of the Russian police, which had been in the offing, "is not now to be feared, according to the French authorities. The socialist parliamentarians have other business on hand at the moment."

decoding

But what if the revolutionaries wrote their letters in code? Then the Okhrana turned them over to a genial research worker who decoded the message. And I am assured that he never failed. This outstanding specialist, whose name was Zybin, had gained such a reputation for infallibility that when the March revolution came . . . he was kept on. He went over to the service of the new government, which I believe employed him in counterespionage.

The most varied kinds of code can apparently be deciphered. A calculation of probabilities gives some clue, whether the combinations used are geometrical or arithmetical. One starting point—the smallest key—is enough to decipher a message. To write the letters, I am told, some comrades used to use certain books in which they had previously agreed to mark off given pages. A good psychologist, Zybin found the books and the pages. "Codes based on texts by well-known writers, on a pattern given in the manuals of the revolutionary organizations, following vertical lines of numbers or letters" are worthless, writes ex-policeman M.E. Bakai.[11] Central codes of organizations are most frequently given away by provocateurs, or cracked by long, minute and precise work. Bakai considers the best codes in common use are those based on less well-known printed works. Zybin had made himself a whole cabinet of catalogue drawers and files, in which it was possible immediately to find, for example, the name of all the towns in Russia with a Saint Alexander Street; the name of all the towns with such and such a factory or school; the real names and pseudonyms of all the suspect persons living in the Empire, etc. He had alphabetical lists of students, sailors, officers, etc. He would find in a seemingly innocent letter the simple words. "'Blackie' sent down High Street tonight," and further down a phrase referring to a "medical student." He had only to look up a few of his registers to see if "Blackie" was already on the files, and which town with a faculty of medicine had a High Street. Three or four clues of this kind set him on the track.

With all the monitored or intercepted correspondence,

the slightest allusions to particular people were transferred to files, with numbers referring back to the text of the letters. Whole archives were filled with such letters. Three completely ordinary letters, coming from revolutionaries scattered across a region, and making incidental reference to a fourth, could give him away completely.

It should be stressed: the interception of correspondence by the secret agencies — whose existence, as a matter of strictly observed custom, is totally denied by the police, but without which there is no police — is of great importance.

The mail of known or suspected persons is opened in the first instance; then there is also a random selection of letters bearing "please forward" on the envelope, others with the envelope addressed in a particular way — those, in a word, which attract attention. The opening of letters at random provides as much useful documentation as the interception of the mail of known revolutionaries. The latter in fact do try to write with caution (although the only worthwhile precaution is really not to mention in letters, even indirectly, anything to do with action), while the ordinary members of the party — the unknown ones — forget the most elementary precautions.

The Okhrana made three copies of letters of interest: one for the mail-opening office, one for police General Headquarters and the other for the local police. The letter would reach its destination. In some cases — for example where invisible ink had to be chemically processed — the police kept the original and sent the addressee a perfectly forged copy, done by another specialist who was a real virtuoso.

The letters were opened by means which varied according to the inventiveness of those doing the job: steaming open envelopes, unpeeling lacquered seals (and then replacing them) with heated razor blades, etc. Most often the corners of the envelope are not well sealed. A tool made from a little strip of metal is then slid into the opening, and the letter gently rolled round it, so that it can easily be taken out and put back in without opening the envelope.

The letters intercepted were never handed over to the courts, in order not to shed the least light, even indirectly, on the work of the mail-opening office. They were used purely for making police reports.

The decoding office not only worked on the revolutionaries' codes. It also collected photographic copies of the diplomatic codes of the great powers . . .

summarizing reports

So far we have only looked at the observation techniques of the Russian police. The procedures are the same whether for an organization, or an individual militant. They proceed in a sense analytically: investigating, noting down, compiling records. After a certain time — possibly a very short time — the police have in their possession four kinds of information on the enemy:

1. Information from external surveillance (tailing), the results of which are summed up in analytical diagrams, to shed light on the enemy's activities and movements, habits, acquaintances, circle, etc.

2. Information from the secret service, or from informers on his or her ideas, intentions, work, clandestine activity
3. The information which can be gleaned from a very careful reading of the revolutionary press and publications
4. Finally, information from the individual's correspondence, or the correspondence of others with him or her, completes the whole

The degree of accuracy of the information gained by the secret agents of course varied. The general impression the files give is nonetheless of a very high level of accuracy, especially in relation to firmly established organizations. The police reports contain detailed minutes of every secret meeting, summaries of each important speech, copies of every clandestine publication, even the duplicated ones.[12]

We already have the police in possession of abundant information. The work of observation and analysis is done. Following the scientific method, the work of classification and synthesis now begins.

The results are laid out in diagrams.

Let's unfold one of them. It is entitled, "Connections of Boris Savinkov."

This diagram, on a sheet two feet by three feet, sums up, so that they can be taken in at a glance, all the data obtained on the terrorist's connections.

In the center is a rectangle, in the form of a visiting card, with his name in handwriting. From this rectangle lines spread out linking it to little colored circles. Often these are in turn the centers from which other lines go to other circles.

And so on. Even the indirect connections of a man can in this way be grasped at once, whatever the number of the intermediaries, conscious or otherwise, who link him to a given person.

In the diagram of Savinkov's connections, the red circles which represent his "combat" connections, are divided into three groups of nine, eight and six people, all denoted by name and patronymic. The green circles represent the people with whom he is, or was in direct contact, political or other (thirty-seven of them); nine yellow circles represent his relatives; the brown circles represent people connected with his friends and acquaintances . . . All this is in Petrograd. Other signs show his connections in Kiev. Reading it, we see for example:

BS knew Barbara Eduardovna Varkhovskaya, who in turn knew twelve people in Petrograd (names and patronymics, etc.) and five in Kiev. It may well be that BS knew nothing of the twelve and the five. But the police knew who was around him better than he did!

In the case of an organization—let's take a series of working diagrams, obviously sketches, of a Socialist Revolutionary organization in the province of Vilna. The red circles form, here and there, something like constellations: the lines between them crisscross to an extraordinary degree. We read: Vilna. A red circle: Ivanov, alias "the Old Man," street, house number, profession. An arrow links him to Pavel (same information), with dates showing that on February 23 (4–5 p.m.), on the 27th (at 9 p.m.) and on the 28th (at 4 p.m.) Ivanov called on Pavel. Another arrow links him to Marfa, who visited him at midday on the 27th.

And so it goes on, with these lines crossing each other like footsteps in the street. It is a table on which you can follow, hour by hour, the activity of an organization.

forensic evidence

A very useful accessory method of the police should be mentioned here: forensic study (or *bertillonage*, after Monsieur Bertillon who invented the system), which is very useful for all legal identification purposes. A forensic file is compiled on every arrested person: he is photographed from every angle, from in front, in profile, standing, sitting; measured with the aid of precision instruments (shape and dimension of the skull, the forearm, the foot, hand, etc.), examined by experts who classify him scientifically (according to the shape of nose and ear, color of eyes, scars or marks on the body). His fingerprints are taken; a study of the slightest curves on the skin's surface can be used, almost infallibly, to detect a person from prints left on a glass or doorknob. In all court cases the forensic files, classified by characteristic signs, supply their quota of information.

The simplest descriptions can be just as dangerous. The angle of an ear, the color of someone's eyes, or the shape of the nose can be observed in the street without alerting their attention. These data will be enough for the experienced policeman to identify his man, in spite of changes he may have been able to make in his appearance. A few prearranged letters will send a scientific description over the telegraph wires.

By now the main revolutionaries are perfectly well known. The police are very well informed about the organization as a whole. All that is left is to make a synthesis, this time concretely. Let's make a good job of it! And they do: in colored diagrams, as careful and as artistically labeled as the work of an architect. The symbols are explained by keys. There is a plan of the organization of the Socialist Revolutionary Party, such as not even the members of its own Central Committee possessed; or diagrams showing the organization of the Polish Socialist Party, the Jewish Bund, propaganda in the Petrograd factories, etc. All the parties and groups are thoroughly studied.

And not in a platonic way either! We are getting closer to the goal. An elegant drawing reveals to us the "Plan for the liquidation of the Social Democratic organization of Riga."

At the top the Central Committee (four names) and the propaganda committee (two names); below, the Riga Committee, linked with 5 groups, with 26 subgroups under them. In all, 76 names in some 30 units. The only thing left to do is to seize them all in one fell swoop and that will be the end of the whole Social Democratic organization of Riga.

an analysis of the revolutionary movement

Once the work was done, those responsible felt a legitimate pride in preserving a record of it. They produced what was virtually a deluxe album of photographs of members of the liquidated organization. I have in front of me the album on the liquidation of the anarcho-communist group, the Communards, by the Moscow police, in August 1910. Four pictures show the group's arms and equipment; there follow 18 portraits accompanied by biographical details.

The materials — the reports, files, diagrams, etc. — which up to now have been used for an immediate, practical purpose, from now on are going to be used, in a certain sense, in a scientific spirit.

Each year, the Okhrana published a book purely for its own employees, containing a succinct but complete account of the main cases which had occurred and reports on the current situation of the revolutionary movement.

Voluminous treatises were written on the revolutionary movement for the instruction of new generations of policemen. The history of each party, its origins and development, can be read with a summary of its ideas and program, a series of drawings accompanied by explanatory texts showing a plan of the organization, the resolutions of its most recent meetings and information on the better-known members. In short, a brief and complete monograph. The history of the anarchist movement in Russia, for example, will be extraordinarily dif-ficult to reconstruct because of the dispersal of members and groups which took place, the unprecedented losses of this movement during the revolution and finally its disintegration. Nonetheless, we have the good fortune to find in the police archives an excellent, very detailed little volume which sums up this history. It would only take the addition of a few notes and a short preface, and the public would find it a book of very great interest.

On the larger parties, the Okhrana published thorough works, some of which would be worth reprinting and, taken together, will at some point be very useful: *On the Jewish Zionist Movement*, 156 pages, large format. Report to the Chief

of Police. *The Activity of the Social Democracy during the War,*
102 closely printed pages. *The Position of the Socialist Revolutionary Party in 1908,* etc. These are some of the titles chosen
at random among the pamphlets produced on the presses of
the imperial police.

The Police Department also brought out periodical news-
sheets for the information of the higher-ranking officers.

For the use of the czar a single-copy edition was made up
of a kind of manuscript review, appearing twelve or fifteen
times a year, and recording the slightest incidents concerning
the revolutionary movement—isolated arrests, successful raids,
acts of repression, disturbances. Nicholas II took it all in. He did
not look down on the information gained by the mail-opening
service. The reports are often annotated in his own hand.

The Okhrana kept watch not only on the enemies of the
autocracy. It was considered a good idea to keep its friends
too in hand, and especially to know what they were thinking.
The mail openers made a special examination of the letters
of high officials, state councilors, ministers, courtesans and
generals, etc. The passages of interest in these letters, listed
by date and subject, formed a thick duplicated volume by
the end of each quarter, and were read only by two or three
powerful persons. General Z's wife wrote to Princess T that
she disapproved of the nomination of Monsieur So-and-So
to the Imperial Council, and that people were making fun of
Minister X in the salons. This was noted down. A minister
makes a comment on a bill, a death, a speech. Copied and
noted down. Under the heading "Information on public
opinion."

protection of the czar's person

The protection of the sacred person of the czar required a special apparatus. I have read some thirty pamphlets on how to prepare His Imperial Majesty's travels by land, sea, rail or car, in the camps, the countryside, the streets. Countless rules governed the organization of every trip the sovereign made. When he had to pass through certain streets on a procession, the itinerary was studied house by house, window by window, in order to know exactly who lived along the route and who visited them. Plans were made of all the houses, and all the streets the cortege would pass down; drawings were made of the housefronts showing the number of flats, the names of the tenants, etc., to enable the police to find their way around.

Several times, in spite of this, Nicholas II's life was in the hands of the terrorists. It was chance circumstances that saved him — not the Okhrana.

the cost of an execution

In among all the red tape and paperwork of the czarist police there abound the saddest of human documents, as we have already seen. Although it is a little outside our subject, I think we should devote a few lines to a series of simple receipts for small sums of money, found enclosed in one of the files. Especially as these little slips of paper appear all too often after the "liquidation" of revolutionary groups, swelling the files already crammed with details of surveillance and informing. As a kind of epilogue . . .

These are the documents which tell us how much an execution cost the czarist judicial system. They are the receipts signed by all those who collaborated, directly or indirectly, with the hangman.

All in all, not very expensive. The sums to the priest and the doctor are especially modest. The priesthood of the one and the profession of the other after all surely imply devotion to humanity.

At this point we should perhaps have a chapter headed: "Torture." All police forces resort in varying degrees to medieval "interrogation." In the United States they practice the terrible "third degree." In most European countries, torture has become generalized because of the resurgence of the class struggle following the war. The Romanian security services, the Polish Defense Ministry, the German, Italian, Yugoslavian, Spanish and Bulgarian police—and there must be others we have missed out—frequently resort to it. The Russian Okhrana preceded them in this, though with a certain degree of moderation. Although there were cases, even many cases, of corporal punishment (the knout) in the prisons, the treatment the Russian police meted out to prisoners before the 1905 revolution seems to have been generally more humane than is the case today when workers are arrested in any one of a dozen European countries. After 1905, the Okhrana had torture chambers in Warsaw, Riga, Odessa and apparently in most of the great urban centers.

Expenses for the execution of the brothers Modat and Djavat Mustapha Ogli, sentenced to death by the court-martial of the Caucasus

Expenses	Cost in rubles
Transportation of the condemned men from the Metek fortress to the prison, paid to the carters	4
Other expenses	4
For having dug and filled in two graves (six grave diggers each signed a receipt for 2 rubles)	12
For setting up the gallows	4
For supervising the job	8
Traveling expenses for a priest (return)	2
To the doctor, for the death certificate	2
To the hangman	50
Hangman's traveling expenses	2

conclusion:
why the Russian Revolution was still invincible

The police had to see everything, know, understand and have power over everything. The strength and perfection of their machinery appears all the more terrible because of the unsuspected resources they dragged up from the depth of the human soul.

But nonetheless they were powerless to prevent what happened. For half a century they vainly defended the autocracy against the revolution, which grew stronger every year.

It would in fact be wrong to let oneself be taken in by the

apparently perfect mechanism of czarist security. It is true that at the top there were some intelligent men, technicians of high professional standing; but the whole machine rested on the work of a mass of ignorant civil servants. In the best-prepared reports some quite amusing discrepancies appear. Money oiled the wheels of this enormous machine; and gain is a strong but inadequate stimulus. Nothing great is achieved without disinterestedness. And the autocracy had no disinterested supporters.

Should it still, after the overthrow of March 26, 1917, be necessary to demonstrate, with facts taken from the history of the Russian Revolution, that the efforts of the head of the Police Department were in vain, we could quote a whole number of arguments like that put forward by the ex-policeman M.E. Bakai. In 1906, after the suppression of the first revolution, when the Chief of Police, Trusevich, re-organized the Okhrana, the revolutionary organizations of Warsaw, and in particular the Polish Socialist Party,[13] in the course of the year liquidated 20 military, 7 constables and 56 policemen and wounded 92; in all, they put 179 officers out of action. They also destroyed 149 consignments of excise alcohol. In the preparation of these actions hundreds of men took part, most of them remaining unknown to the police. M.E. Bakai observes that, in periods of revolutionary upsurge, agents provocateurs often lay low; but they reappeared as reaction gained the upper hand, like carrion crows over the battlefields.

In 1917, the autocracy fell without the legions of in-formers, provocateurs, hangmen, policemen, civil guards, cossacks, judges, generals and priests being able to deflect the unswerving course of history. The reports from the Okhrana, written by General Globachev, affirm that the revolution is close at hand and offer the czar vain warnings. Just as the most knowledgeable doctors called to a deathbed can only observe, minute by minute, the progress of the disease, the omniscient police of the Empire watched impotently as the world of czarism plunged into the abyss.

For the revolution was the outcome of economic, psychological and moral causes outside their reach. They were doomed to resist helplessly and then succumb. Because it is the eternal illusion of the ruling classes to think that they can remove the effects without getting to the causes, legislate against anarchy or against syndicalism (as in France and the United States), against socialism (as Bismarck did in Germany), or against communism, as they strive to do more or less everywhere today. The same old historical experience. The Roman Empire too persecuted the Christians in vain. Catholicism had people burned at the stake throughout Europe, without defeating the heresy which is the essence of life.

In fact, the Russian police were overtaken by history. Instinctively, or consciously, the overwhelming majority of the population gave their sympathy to the enemies of the *ancien régime*. Their frequent martyrdom brought them some recruits and the admiration of countless others. Among the people, Christians for long centuries, there was an irresistible attraction towards the apostolic life of the propagandists who, renouncing comfort and security, faced prison, Siberian exile and death itself to bring the new evangel to the oppressed. They were the real "salt of the earth": they were the best, the only bearers of an immense hope, and for this they were persecuted.

On their side they had the only moral strength, the strength of ideas and feelings. The autocracy was no longer a living principle. No one believed it was necessary. It no longer had any ideologues. Even religion, in the voices of its most sincere thinkers, condemned a regime which now rested solely on the systematic use of violence. The greatest Christians of modern Russia, the Dukhobors and Tolstoyans, were anarchists. But a society which no longer rests on living ideals, and whose basic principles are dead, often survives for a time by sheer weight of inertia.

But in Russian society in the last years of the *ancien régime*, the new, subversive ideas had acquired irresistible force. Everyone in the working class, the petty bourgeoisie, the army and the navy, the liberal professions—everyone who acted and thought—was a revolutionary, that is, a "socialist" of some kind. There was no satisfied middle bourgeoisie as in the countries of Western Europe. The *ancien régime* was no longer really defended by anyone except the upper clergy, the court nobility, the financiers, and a few politicians, in other words, by a very small aristocracy. Revolutionary ideas therefore found fertile soil everywhere. Over a long period, the nobility and the bourgeoisie gave the flower of their youth to the revolution. When a revolutionary went into hiding, he found many spontaneous, disinterested, devoted helpers. When he was arrested it happened more and more frequently that the soldiers in charge of conveying him sympathized with him, and among the jailers he sometimes found "comrades." So much so that in most prisons it was easy to communicate illegally with the outside world. This sympathy

the big landowner, the rural masses, after over half a century, enthusiastically greeted the call of the revolutionaries who had forsaken their class: "Peasants, seize the land!" And as these masses supplied the army with the overwhelming majority of its ranks, the cannon fodder for Lyaoyang and Mukden, and the scourge of all uprisings, the army, with the military organizations of the clandestine parties working within it—this army kept in obedience by the courts-martial and the "gagging regime"—was in a ferment of bitterness. A working class still young, multiplying as fast as capitalist industry developed, deprived of consciousness, organizations, a press (rights not recognized by the old regime in Russia), oblivious to the attraction of the parliamentary regime, living in hovels, on low wages, the target of arbitrary police action—in short, faced with the bare reality of the class struggle—this working class became more and more clearly conscious of its interests with every day that passed. Thirty nationalities conquered or annexed by the Empire, deprived of the elemental right of speaking their own languages, or of the possibility of maintaining their own culture, Russified under the whip, were only kept under the yoke by constant repressive measures. In Poland, in Finland, in the Ukraine and the Baltic countries, in the Caucasus, national revolutions were in gestation, preparing to join forces with the agrarian revolution, the workers' revolution, the bourgeois revolution. The Jewish question was coming up everywhere too.

Holding the reins of power was a degenerate dynasty surrounded by imbeciles. The hairdresser Philip treated the shaky health of the heir presumptive by hypnotism. From his private council rooms, Rasputin removed and set up ministries. The generals robbed from the army, the high dignitaries plundered the state. Between this power and the nation stood a countless bureaucracy, well oiled with bribes.

In the midst of the masses were the revolutionary organizations, broad-based and disciplined, constantly active, possessing both vast experience and the prestige and support of a magnificent tradition.

Such were the profound forces working for the revolution. And it was against them, in the vain hope of stemming the avalanche, that the Okhrana stretched its spindly strands of barbed wire!

In this deplorable situation, the police worked skillfully. Fair enough. They would manage, for example, to "liquidate" the Riga Social Democratic organization. Seventy would be taken prisoner, beheading the movement in the area. Imagine for one moment what total "liquidation" means. No one escaped. And then?

For a start, the imprisonment of the 70 did not go unnoticed. Each of the members was in contact with at least 10 people. Seven hundred people, at least, were suddenly faced with the brutal fact of the seizure of honest, brave people, whose only crime was to strive for the common good. The trial, the sentences, the private dramas involved, brought about an explosion of interest and support for the revolutionaries. If even one of them was able to make his impassioned voice heard from the dock, it could be said with certainty that the organization, at the sound of this voice, would rise again from the ashes. It was only a question of time.

And then what was to be done with the 70 members in prison? They could only be locked up for a long time or deported to the deserted regions of Siberia. Very good. But in prison — or in Siberia — they find comrades, teachers and pupils. Their enforced leisure obliges them to study, to shape their theoretical ideas. Suffering together, they grow harder, become tempered, impassioned. Sooner or later, escaping, amnestied — through general strikes — or paroled, they will return to the life of society as "veteran" revolutionaries, "illegal" this time, and much stronger than ever. Not all of them of course. Some of them will die on the way; a painful selection process, useful in its own way. And the memories of friends who disappeared will make those who survive intransigent.

In the end, a liquidation is never completely final. The precautions of the revolutionaries will preserve some. The interests of provocation in themselves require some of the prisoners to be liberated. And chance operates in the same way. The ones who "escaped," although they find themselves in difficult situations, are soon able to take advantage of favorable circumstances . . .

Repression can only really live off fear. But is fear enough to remove need, thirst for justice, intelligence, reason, idealism — all those revolutionary forces that express the formidable, profound impulse of the economic factors of a revolution? Relying on intimidation, the reactionaries forget that they will cause more indignation, more hatred, more thirst for martyrdom, than real fear. They only intimidate the weak; they exasperate the best forces and temper the resolution of the strongest.

And the provocateurs?

At first sight, they can cause the revolutionary movement terrible losses. But is this really so?

Due to their help, the police can, of course, multiply their arrests and the "liquidation" of groups. In given circumstances, they can counter the most carefully laid political plans. They can do away with valiant militants. Provocateurs have often been the direct suppliers of the hangman. This is, of course, all terrible, but it is also the case that provocation can only wipe out individuals or groups and that it is almost impotent against the revolutionary movement as a whole.

We have seen how an agent provocateur became responsible (in 1912) for bringing Bolshevik propaganda into Russia; how another (Malinovsky) gave speeches written by Lenin in the Duma; how a third organized the execution of Plehve. In the first case, our agent could hand over a considerable quantity of literature to the police; but nonetheless he could not, for fear of blowing his cover at once, hand over all the literature, or even more than a limited quantity. Willy-nilly, he did contribute to the circulation. Whether a propaganda leaflet is handed out by a secret agent or a devoted revolutionary, the results are still the same; the essential thing is that it should be read. Whether Plehve's execution was prepared by Azev or Savinkov doesn't matter to us. It does not even matter whether it was the result of a struggle between different factions of the police; the important thing is that Plehve disappeared. The interests of the revolution in this case are much more important than those of the wretched little Machiavellis of the Okhrana. When the secret agent Malinovsky acted as Lenin's voice in the Duma, the Minister of the Interior was wrong to rejoice over the success of his hired agent. Lenin's words were far more important to the country than the mere voice of a wretch like him. We can, thus, give two definitions of an agent which are complementary, but of which the second is much more significant:

1. The agent provocateur is a fake revolutionary
2. The agent provocateur is a policeman who serves the revolution in spite of himself — because he must always appear to be serving it

But in this question there are no appearances. Propaganda, fighting, terrorism, is all reality. There is no way you can be a member halfway, or superficially.

Wretches who in a moment of cowardice threw themselves into this swamp paid for it. Recently, in his *Untimely Thoughts*, Maxim Gorki published a curious letter from an agent provocateur. What the man wrote was something like this: "I was conscious of my baseness, but I also knew that it could not for a single second hold back the triumph of the revolution."

What is certain is that provocation poisons the struggle. It incites people to terrorism, even to terrorism of a type revolutionaries prefer to abstain from. What is really to be done with a traitor? The idea of pardoning him occurs to no one. In the duel between the police and the revolutionaries, provocation adds an element of intrigue, suffering, hatred and contempt. Is it more dangerous to the revolution than to the police? I think not. From another standpoint, the provocateurs and the police have a direct interest in ensuring that the revolutionary movement, which is their *raison d'être*, should always be a threat. In case of need, rather than give up a second source of earnings, they hatch plots themselves, as we have seen. In such cases, the interests of the police are completely in contradiction with those of the regime which it is their job to defend. The maneuvers of such provocateurs can in a certain sense also be dangerous to the state itself. Azev once organized an attempt on the czar's life, which was frustrated only by totally fortuitous and unforeseen circumstances (one of the revolutionaries renouncing the plan). At that instant, Azev's personal interest — which was undoubtedly much dearer to him than the security of the Empire — demanded a bold action; within the Socialist Revolutionary Party he was under a cloud of suspicion which placed his life in danger. On the other hand, it has been raised that the attacks he successfully carried out might have served the designs of some Fouché. It is possible. But such intrigues among those in power only reveal the gangrene of a regime and contribute in no small measure to its fall.

Provocation is much more dangerous in terms of the distrust it sows among revolutionaries. As soon as a few traitors are unmasked, trust disappears from within the organizations. It is a terrible thing, because confidence in the party is the cement of all revolutionary forces. Accusations are murmured about, then said out loud, and usually they cannot be checked out. This causes enormous damage, worse in some ways than that caused by provocation itself. Recall these harrowing cases: Barbès made an accusation against the heroic Blanqui — and Blanqui, in spite of his forty years of solitary confinement, in spite of his exemplary life and his indomitability, could never get rid of the infamous slander. Bakunin was also accused. And what about the victims who were less well known, but not less harmed by slander? Girier-Lorion, the anarchist, was accused of provocation by the "socialist" deputy Delory; to free himself of this intolerable suspicion, he shot the agents and was taken off to die in prison. Another who met the same fate was also a valiant anarchist, from Belgium: Hartenstein-Sokolov (of the Ghent trial of 1909), who was vilely smeared by the whole socialist press and died in prison as a result. There is a tradition of it: the enemies of action, the cowards, the well entrenched ones, the opportunists, are happy to assemble their arsenal — in the sewers! Suspicion and slander are their weapons for discrediting revolutionaries. And we have not seen the end of it yet.

This evil of suspicion and mistrust among us can only be reduced and isolated by a great effort of will. It is necessary, as the condition of any victorious struggle against real provocation — and slanderous accusation of members is playing the game of provocation — that no one should be accused lightly, and it should also be impossible for an accusation against a revolutionary to be accepted without being investigated. Every time anyone is touched by suspicion, a jury formed of comrades should determine whether it is a well-founded accusation or a slander. These are simple rules which should be observed with inflexible rigor if one wishes to preserve the moral health of revolutionary organizations.

And what is more, however dangerous it is for the individuals concerned, the strength of the agent provocateur should not be overestimated: to a large extent, it is also up to every member to defend himself properly.

The Russian revolutionaries, in their long struggle against the police of the *ancien régime*, had acquired a very sure, practical knowledge of the procedures and methods of the police. If the police were very strong, they were stronger still. Whatever the perfection of the tables drawn up by the

Okhrana specialists on the activity of a given organization, it is certain that it contains gaps. As we said, "liquidation" of a group was rarely complete, because through their precautions, someone would escape. In the highly laborious diagram of Boris Savinkov's connections, some names are missing; and perhaps the most important ones. The Russian revolutionaries in fact considered that clandestine (illegal) action was subject to unbending rules. At every turn they asked themselves: "Is this in line with the rules of conspiracy?"[14] The "code of conspiracy" had outstanding theoreticians and practitioners among the great enemies of the autocracy and of capital in Russia. It would be extremely useful to study this in depth. It must contain the simplest rules, precisely those which, because they are so simple, are often forgotten.

Thanks to this science of conspiracy, the revolutionaries were able to live illegally in the main cities of Russia for months or years at a time. They were able to turn themselves, as the case required, into peddlers, coachmen, "rich foreigners," servants, etc. In each case they had to live out their roles. To blow up the Winter Palace, the worker Stepan Khalturin[15] spent weeks living the life of the workers employed at the palace. In order to keep watch on Plehve in Petrograd, Kaliaev became a coachman. Lenin and Zinoviev, hunted by Kerensky's police, were able to find a hiding place in Petrograd and only went out in disguise—Lenin as a factory worker.

Illegal action, over a period, creates habits and an outlook which can be considered the best guarantee against police methods. What talented police, what clever impostors can be compared with revolutionaries who are sure of themselves, circumspect, thoughtful and valiant, who obey a common watchword?

Whatever the perfection of the methods used by the police to keep track of revolutionaries, won't there always be an irreducible unknown in their movements and actions? Won't there always be, in the most carefully worked out equations of the enemy, an enormous, fearful "x"? What traitor, what skilled informer or spy can decipher revolutionary intelligence? Who can measure the strength of revolutionary will?

When you have on your side the laws of history, the interests of the future, the economic and moral needs which lead to revolution; when you know with certainty what you want, what arms you have and what the enemy has; when you have decided on illegal action; when you have confidence in yourself and you work only with those in whom you have confidence; when you know that revolutionary work demands sacrifices and that every lovingly sown seed will bear fruit a hundred times over, then you are invincible.

The proof of this is that the thousands of Okhrana files, the millions of notes from the information services, the magnificent diagrams by its technicians, the works of its scientists, the whole amazing arsenal, is now in the hands of the Russian communists. The police, on the day of revolt, fled the cries of the crowd; those who were caught by the coattails took a dive—for good—into the canals of Petrograd. In the main, the officers of the Okhrana were shot.[16] All the provocateurs who could be identified met the same fate. And one day, partly to show to the foreign comrades, we set up in a kind of museum a number of particularly interesting items taken from the secret archives of the police of the Empire. Our exhibition took place in one of the finest halls of the Winter

Palace; the visitors could leaf through, by a window between two malachite columns, the jail book of the Peter and Paul Prison, the somber Bastille of the czars, over whose ancient battlements, on the other side of the river Neva, they could see the red flag flying.

Those who saw it know that even before it has conquered, the revolution is invincible.

2 THE PROBLEM OF ILLEGALITY

don't be fooled

Without a clear perspective on this problem, knowledge of police methods and procedures would be of no practical utility.

Fetishism of legality was and still is one of the characteristic features of the class collaboration tendency of socialism. It involves a belief in the possibility of transforming the capitalist order without entering into conflict with its privileged elements. But rather than indicating a naiveté quite incompatible with the mentality of politicians, it is a sign of the corruption of the leaders. Entrenched in a society they pretend to be fighting, they recommend respecting the rules of the game. The working class can only respect bourgeois legality if it ignores the real role of the state and the deceptive nature of democracy; in short, the first principles of the class struggle.

If the worker knows that the state is a mesh of institutions designed to defend the interests of the property owners against the non-owners, that is, to maintain the exploitation of labor; that the law, always decreed by the rich against the poor, is enforced by magistrates invariably belonging to the ruling class; that the law is invariably enforced along rigorous class lines; that coercion, which begins with a quiet order from a policeman, passes via the lockup and the penitentiary, and ends with the fall of the guillotine—is the systematic exercise of legalized violence against the exploited, then the only way the worker can view legality is as a fact, whose different facets he should know about, with its different applications, traps and pitfalls (and also advantages, which should be made use of at certain points) but which should be nothing but a purely material obstacle to his class.

Is it necessary to demonstrate the antiproletarian nature of all bourgeois legality? Perhaps. In our unequal struggle against the old world, the simplest things must be explained again and again each day. We need only mention a number of fairly well-known facts.

In every country, the workers' movement has had to win, in over half a century of struggle, the right to associate and the right to strike. Even in France this right is still not conceded to state employed workers nor those in industries considered to be of public utility (as if all industries aren't), such as the railways.

In the conflicts between capital and labor, the army has often intervened against labor—never against capital.

In court the defense of the poor is nothing short of impossible, because of the cost of any judicial action; in effect, a worker can neither bring a case nor defend one.

The overwhelming majority of crimes are directly caused by poverty and come into the category of attacks on property. The overwhelming majority of prison inmates are from the poor.

Up until the war, there was discriminatory suffrage in Belgium; a capitalist, a curate, an officer or a lawyer each had as many votes as two, or three workers. At the time of writing an attempt is being made to reestablish discriminatory suffrage in Italy.

To respect legality such as this is to be fooled by it. Nonetheless, it would be equally disastrous to ignore it. The advantages for the workers' movement are the greater the less one is fooled. The right to exist and to act legally is, for the organizations of the proletariat, something which must constantly be re-won and extended. We stress this because sometimes among good revolutionaries there emerges the diametrical opposite of fetishizing legality — due to a kind of tendency to make the least political effort (it is easier to conspire than to lead mass action) they have a certain disdain for legal action.

We believe that in countries where the reaction has not yet triumphed, destroying the previous democratic constitution, the workers will have to fight to defend every inch of their legal position, and in other countries fight to regain it. In France itself, the legal status the workers' movement enjoys must be extended, and this can only be done through struggle. The right of association and the right to strike are still denied to state employees and certain other categories of workers; the right to demonstrate is much more restricted than in the Anglo-Saxon countries; the advanced guard of workers' defense have still not conquered the streets and gained legality as in Germany and Austria.

the postwar experience

During the war the governments of all the belligerent countries replaced democratic institutions by military dictatorship (martial law, the virtual suppression of the right to strike, prorogation or recess of parliaments, handing over all power to the generals and the court-martial regimes). The exceptional requirements of national defense gave them a plausible justification. Since the end of the war, when the Red tide surging out from Russia flowed out over the whole of Europe, almost all the capitalist states — this time fighting the class war, and under threat from the workers' movement — treated their previously sacred legislation as worth less than the paper it was written on.

The Baltic states (Finland, Estonia, Lithuania, Latvia) and Poland, Romania and Yugoslavia brought out against the working class brutal laws untainted with democratic hypocrisy. Bulgaria refined the effects of its brutal legislation with extra-legal violence. Hungary, Italy and Spain were content with abolishing, so far as the workers and peasants were concerned, any legality whatsoever. More cultivated, and better organized, Germany, without resorting to special powers, established what can be called a regime of legal police terror.[1] The United States brutally applies its laws on "criminal unionism," sabotage and . . . espionage! Thousands of workers were arrested under an Espionage Act passed during the war against German subjects living in the United States.

The only countries left in Europe where the labor movement still enjoys the benefits of democratic legality are Scandinavia, England, France and a few small countries. It can be said without fear of being disproved by events that with the first really dangerous social crisis this advantage will be promptly and abruptly withdrawn. Very definite signs have appeared which demand our attention. In November 1924, the British elections took place on the basis of an anticommunist campaign, the basic evidence for which was a forged letter from Zinoviev, supposedly addressed to the British Labour Party and intercepted by the state. In France there have on several occasions been attempts to dissolve the CGT. If I am not mistaken, this dissolution even received formal approval. Briand in his time even—illegally—went so far as to militarize railway workers, in order to break their strike. Clemenceau's tactics are not something belonging to the distant past—and Poincaré has shown, since the occupation of the Ruhr, an evident desire to imitate him.

Now, for a revolutionary party, being taken unawares by being outlawed means that you disappear. On the other hand, being prepared for illegality makes you certain of surviving any measures of repression. Three striking examples from recent history illustrate the truth of this.

1. A great communist party which allowed itself to be taken unawares when made illegal:

   The Yugoslav Communist Party, a mass party, which in 1920 had more than 120,000 members and sixty deputies in the Skupchina, was dissolved in 1921, in compliance with the State Defense Law. Its defeat was instant and total. It disappeared from the political scene.[2]

2. A communist party which was taken only half unawares:

The Italian Communist Party [PCI] was obliged, even before Mussolini's rise to power, to pursue what was at best a semi-legal existence, because of fascist persecution. The furious repression—with 4,000 workers arrested in the first week of 1923— was at no point able to smash the PCI, which on the contrary was strengthened and fortified, its membership rising from 10,000 in 1923 to almost 30,000 at the beginning of 1925.

3. A great communist party which was not in the least taken unawares:

At the end of 1923, after the revolutionary events of October and the Hamburg insurrection, the German Communist Party was dissolved by General von Seeckt. Prepared over a long period, and with flexible, illegal organizations, it was none-theless able to continue its normal existence. The government soon had to reconsider a measure of such evident inanity. The German Communist Party came out of illegality with its forces hardly impaired, to get over three and a half million votes in the 1924 elections.

the limits of legal revolutionary action

What is more, legality, in the most "advanced" capitalist democracies, has limits which the proletariat cannot respect without condemning itself to defeat. Propaganda in the army, a vital necessity, is not legally tolerated. Without the defection of at least a part of the army, there is no victorious revolution. This is a law of history. In every bourgeois army, the party of the proletariat must arouse and cultivate revolutionary traditions, possess extensive organizations, tenacious in their work, and more vigilant than the enemy. The most democratic of legal systems would not in the least tolerate action committees at the very points where they are most necessary: in the great railway junctions, the docks, the arsenals and the airports. The most democratic of legal systems does not tolerate communist propaganda in the colonies: as proof, take the persecution of the Egyptian and Indian revolutionaries by the British authorities; and also the regime of police provocation established by the French authorities in Tunisia. Finally, it need scarcely be said that international communications services must at all times be subject to investigation by the political police.

Nobody maintained the need for illegal revolutionary organization more firmly than Lenin—in the period of the founding of the Russian Bolshevik Party and later, during the founding of the European communist parties. Nobody fought harder against the fetishism of legality. At the Second Congress of the Russian Social Democracy (in Brussels and London, 1903), the division between Mensheviks and Bolsheviks took shape precisely over the question of illegal organization. The motive was the discussion of the first paragraph of the statutes. L. Martov, who for 20 years was to be the leader of Menshevism, wanted to concede membership of the party to anyone which lent it his services (under the control of the party)—that is, in reality, to the many sympathizers, especially in intellectual circles, who would try not to compromise themselves to the point of collaborating in illegal actions. Intractably, Lenin maintained that to belong to the party it was necessary "to participate in the work of one of its (illegal) organizations." The discussion appeared to be splitting hairs. But Lenin was a thousand times right. You cannot be half, or a third a revolutionary. The party of the revolution must, of course, make use of every contribution; but it cannot be content with receiving just vague, discreet, verbal, inactive sympathy from its members. Those who do not agree to risk a privileged material situation for the sake of the working class, should not be in a position to exercise real influence within it. The attitude towards illegality was for Lenin the touchstone for differentiating between real revolutionaries and others.[3]

private police forces

Another factor must be taken into account: the existence of private police forces outside the law that provide the bourgeoisie with excellent hired guns.

During the world war, the information service of Action Française was notably successful in supplying Clemenceau's courts-martial. It is well known that Marius Plateau was at the head of AF's private police. Meanwhile, a certain Jean Maxe,[4] the zealous compiler and distributor of the *Cahiers de l'antifrance*, devoted himself to spying on the vanguard movements. It is very likely that all the reactionary formations inspired by the example of the Italian fascists have espionage and police services.

In Germany, since the official disarming of the country, the essential forces of reaction have been concentrated in extremely secretive organizations. The reaction has understood that, even in parties supported by the state, clandestinity is a precious asset. Naturally all these organizations take on the functions of virtual undercover police forces against the proletariat.

In Italy, the fascist party is not content with having the official police at its disposal. It has its own espionage and counterespionage services. Everywhere it spreads informers, secret agents, provocateurs and police spies. And it is this mafia, police and terrorists all in one, which "suppressed" Matteotti—as it had many others.

In the United States, the participation of the private police in the conflicts between labor and capital has grown fearfully. The offices of famous private detectives provide the capitalists with discreet informers, expert provocateurs, riflemen, guards, foremen and also totally corrupt "trade union militants." The Pinkertons, Burns and Thiels detective agencies have 100 head offices and about 10,000 branches: they supposedly employ 135,000 people. Their annual budget comes to $65 million. They have set up industrial espionage, factory-floor espionage, espionage in the workshop, the ship-yards, offices, and wherever there are workers employed. They have created the prototype of the worker-informer.[5]

An analogous system, exposed by Upton Sinclair, operates in the universities and schools of the great democracy whose praises are sung by Walt Whitman.

conclusions

To sum up: the study of the workings of the Okhrana shows us that the immediate aim of the police is more to know than to repress. To know in order to repress at the appointed hour, to the extent desired—if not altogether. Faced by this wily adversary, powerful and cunning, a workers' party lacking clandestine organization, a party which keeps nothing hidden, is like an unarmed man, with no cover, in the sights of a well positioned rifleman. Revolutionary work is too serious to be kept in a glasshouse. The party of the revolution must organize so as to avoid enemy vigilance as far as possible; so as to hide its most important resources absolutely; so as not—in the countries which are still democratic—to be at the mercy of a lurch to the right by the bourgeoisie, or of a declaration of war so as to train our comrades in the behavior which is demanded by these imperatives.[6]

3 SIMPLE ADVICE TO REVOLUTIONARIES

simple advice to revolutionaries

The great Russian Bolsheviks choose to describe themselves as "professional revolutionaries." It is a description perfectly suited to all real agents of social transformation. It rules out from revolutionary activity all dilettantism, amateurism, playing about and posturing; it locates the revolutionary irrevocably in the world of labor, where there is no question of "airs," nor of finding interesting ways to fill up one's leisure time, nor the spiritual, or moral pleasure of holding "advanced" ideas. For those who do this work, their job (or profession) fills the best part of their life. They know it is a serious business and that their daily bread depends on it; they also know, with varying degrees of consciousness, that the whole social life and destiny of humanity depends on it too.

The job of a revolutionary requires a long apprenticeship, gaining purely technical knowledge, as well as love for the work and understanding of the cause, the means and the end. If, as often happens, a person is obliged to take another job—in order to live—it is the job of being a revolutionary which fills that person's life, and the other job is only something secondary. The Russian Revolution was able to triumph because in twenty-five years of political activity it had formed strong teams of professional revolutionaries, trained to carry out an almost superhuman labor.

The truth of this experience must always be borne in mind by any revolutionary worthy of the name. In the present complexity of the class war, the training of a revolutionary needs years of effort, testing out, study and conscious preparation. Every worker spurred on by the desire not to be an insignificant bystander among the exploited masses, but to serve their class and live a fuller life, taking part in the fight to transform society, must endeavor to be also — so far as possible — a professional revolutionary ... And in their party, trade union, or branch work, individuals must — and this is what concerns us today — show themselves to be on their guard against police surveillance and uncover it, even when it is invisible and appears to be innocuous, as it does in periods of calm.

The following recommendations may be very useful in this regard. They are not, however, a complete code of the rules of clandestinity, nor even of precautions to be taken by revolutionaries. They contain no sensational recipe. They are simply basic rules. Strictly speaking, common sense should be enough to suggest them. But unfortunately, long experience teaches us that it is not out of place to spell them out.

Carelessness on the part of revolutionaries has always been the best aid the police have.

being followed

Secret surveillance, following someone, which is the basis of all surveillance, is almost always easy to detect. Every revolutionary must regard himself or herself as being permanently followed: on principle they should never neglect to take the necessary precautions to prevent being followed. In big towns, where there is a lot of traffic, and where there are various means of transport, successful tailing can only be due to culpable negligence on the part of comrades.

The simplest rules are:

- don't go directly to where you are going
- turn down a deserted street to check whether you are being followed
- when in doubt, turn back
- if you notice that you are being followed, jump on some kind of transport, and then change

It is not difficult to "plant" agents in a small town; but when it becomes obvious, such surveillance loses most of its value.

Get rid of the preconceived image of the "secret policeman." Often they are quite easily identifiable. But good "tails" can adapt to any variety of jobs. The most ordinary passerby, the worker in overalls, the street hawker, driver or soldier may be a policeman. Be aware that women, youth, even children may be used for following people. We know of a Russian police circular recommending the use of schoolchildren on missions the police could not carry out without being noticed.

Be on guard also against the tiresome mania for seeing an informer in every passerby.

correspondence and notes

Write down as little as possible. It's better not to write. Don't take notes on sensitive subjects; it's better sometimes to forget certain things than to take them down in writing. With that in mind, practice remembering addresses and especially street numbers by mnemonics.

Notebooks: Where necessary, take notes which are intelligible only to yourself. Everyone can invent ways of abbreviating, and inverting, or transposing numbers (24 for 42; one for g, g for one, etc.). Give your own names to streets, squares, etc., to reduce the margin of error go by association of ideas (Blackie Street will become Dark Street, Thorne will become Prickly, or Spiny, etc.).

Letters: With correspondence, take into account that your mail will be opened. Say as little as possible, and endeavor to make yourself understood only by the addressee. Mention no third persons unless necessary. If it is necessary, remember that a first name is better than a surname, and that an initial — especially a common one — is better than a first name.

Change around your usual addresses.

Avoid all details (about places, work, dates, people, etc.).

Learn to resort, even without prior agreement, to what should always be very simple stratagems for trivializing information. Don't say, for example: "Comrade Peter has been arrested," but "Uncle P. has suddenly fallen ill."

Get letters sent to you through a third person.

Seal letters well. Don't think that wax seals are an absolute guarantee; make them very thin; the thicker ones are easier to lift off.

One good method is to sew the letter into the back of the envelope and cover the thread with an elegant wax seal.

Always remember: "Give me three lines of a man's handwriting and I'll see him swing" is an axiom familiar to all police forces.

general conduct

Beware of telephones. It's the easiest thing for them to tap them.

Telephone conversations between two public phones (in cafés, pay phones, stations) present less problems.

Don't make appointments over the telephone except in prearranged terms.

Get to know places well. Where necessary, study them beforehand. Remember houses, passageways, public places (stations, museums, cafés, stores) with a number of exits.

In public places, on trains, on private visits, be aware of the possibilities of being observed and therefore pay attention to the lighting. Try to see without being seen. It's good where you can to sit behind the light: you can see better and at the same time you're less visible. It is not a good idea to appear at a window.

among comrades

Make it a principle that, in illegal activity, a revolutionary should know only what it is useful for him to know; and that it is often dangerous to know, or to tell more.

The less that is known about a job, the greater its security and its chance of success.

Be on guard against the inclination to give away confidences.

Know how to keep quiet; keeping quiet is a duty to the party, to the revolution.

Know how to forget of your own accord what you should not know.

It is a mistake, which may have serious consequences, to tell your closest friend, girlfriend, or most trusty comrade a party secret which it is not indispensable for them to know. Sometimes you may be doing them wrong; because you are responsible for what you know, and it may be a heavy responsibility.

Don't take offense, or get annoyed at another comrade's silence. This isn't a sign of lack of confidence, but rather of fraternal esteem and of what should be a mutual consciousness of revolutionary duty.

in the event of arrest

At all costs keep cool. Don't let yourself get intimidated, or provoked.

Don't reply to any question without having a defense

counsel present and without previously consulting with him. If possible, he should be a party comrade. If this isn't possible, don't say anything without really thinking about it. In the old days all the revolutionary papers in Russia published, in large type, the constant recommendation: "Comrades, make no statements! Say nothing!"

As a matter of principle: say nothing. Explaining yourself is dangerous; you are in the hands of professionals able to get something out of your every word. Any explanation gives them valuable documentation.

Lying is extremely dangerous: it is difficult to construct a story without its defects being too obvious. It is almost impossible to improvise.

Don't try to be cleverer than them: the relationship of forces is too unequal for that.

Old jailbirds write this strong recommendation on prison walls, for the revolutionary to learn from: "Never confess!"

When you deny anything, deny it firmly.

Remember that the enemy is capable of anything.[1]

Don't let yourself be surprised, or disconcerted by the classic: "We know everything!"

This is never the case. It is a barefaced trick used by all police forces and all examining magistrates with all those under arrest.

Don't be intimidated by the eternal threat: "You'll pay for this!"

What you'll pay for is a confession, or a clumsy explanation, or falling for tricks and moments of panic; but whatever the situation of the accused, a hermetically sealed defense, built on much silence and a few definite affirmations, or denials, can only help.

Don't believe a word of another classic ploy: "We know everything because your Comrade So-and-so has talked!"

Don't believe a word of it, even if they try to prove it. With a few carefully selected clues, the enemy is capable of feigning a profound knowledge of things. Even if So and So did "tell all," this is a further reason to be doubly circumspect.

You know nothing, or as little as possible about the people they are asking about.

In confrontations, keep cool. Don't show surprise. Again: say nothing.

Never sign a document without having read it right through and understood it fully. If you have the slightest doubt, refuse to sign.

If the accusation is groundless — which often happens — don't get indignant: leave it as it is rather than challenge it. Apart from this do nothing without the help of counsel, who should be a comrade.

before judges and police

Don't give way to the inclination instilled by bourgeois idealist education to establish, or reestablish, "the truth."

In the social conflict there is no truth in common between the exploited classes and the exploiters.

There is no truth — great or small — no impersonal, supreme, imperative truth which stands above the class struggle.

For the property owning class, truth is their right: their right to exploit, plunder, legislate, imprison those who want a better future, mercilessly beat down those who spread class consciousness among the proletariat. Any lie which suits them, they call the truth. Scientific truth, say their sociologists, is the eternal nature of individual property (abolished by the soviets). Legal truth is the revolting lie of the equality of rich and poor before the law. Official truth is the impartiality of justice: the arm of one class against the rest.

Their truth is not ours.

Before the judges of the bourgeois class, the revolutionary does not have to account for his or her acts nor respect any so-called truth of theirs. One is forced to appear before them.

One suffers violence. One's only concern, here too, must be the working class. For the working class, one can speak, turn the dock into a rostrum, turn oneself from the accused into the accuser. For the working class, one must also know how to keep silent. Or defend oneself intelligently in order, with one's freedom, to regain the possibility of action.

We owe truth only to our own comrades, our own class, our own party.

Faced with the judges and the police, do not forget that they are the servants of the rich, doing the dirtiest jobs for them.

That if they are the strongest, we are unquestionably right against them.

That they slavishly defend an iniquitous, evil order, doomed by the course of history itself.

Whereas we are working for the only noble cause of our times: the transformation of the world by the emancipation of labor.

ingenuity

The application of these few rules requires a quality every revolutionary should try to cultivate: ingenuity.

A comrade arrives at a watched house and goes up to the fourth floor flat. He barely gets to the stairs, when three suspicious-looking characters start following him. They are going the same way. On the second floor the comrade stops, knocks at a doctor's door and asks about surgery hours. The cops carry on.

Followed in a Petrograd street and about to be apprehended by his pursuers, a revolutionary suddenly darts into a doorway, brandishing an object in his hand. "Watch out—it's a bomb!" The pursuers draw back. The man being followed disappears down a passage: the house has two exits. He gets away. His bomb was nothing but his rolled up hat!

In a country where all communist literature is banned, a bookseller shows a customer John Rockefeller's memoirs: *How I Became a Millionaire.* From the fourth page on, the text is an article by Lenin.

a supreme warning

Be on your guard against conspiracy mania, against posing, adopting airs of mystery, dramatizing simple events, or "conspiratorial" attitudes. The greatest virtue in a revolutionary is simplicity, and scorn for all poses including "revolutionary" and especially conspiratorial poses.

4 THE PROBLEM OF REVOLUTIONARY REPRESSION

machine gun,
typewriter, or . . . ?

"What do you think of the machine gun? Wouldn't you rather
have a typewriter or a camera?"

Decent people, who take a pride in sociology, sometimes
when they are faced with the realities of the revolution, pose
questions of this caliber.

Some of them wax lyrical in disapproval of all violence and
all dictatorship. To put an end to oppression, poverty, prostitution and war, they trust only in the intervention — above
all the literary intervention — of the mind. In fact enjoying
considerable comfort in society as it is, they haughtily place
themselves "above the social melee." What they especially
prefer to the machine gun is the typewriter.

Others, without repudiating violence, formally repudiate
dictatorship. The revolution appears to them to be a miracu-
lous liberation. They dream of a human race made instantly
peaceful and good by the removal of its bonds. They dream,
in defiance of history, truth, common sense and their own
experience, of a total revolution, doubtless not only idyllic,
but short, decisive and definitive, leading to a radiant
morrow. "Fresh and joyous," one would say, so much does
this conception of the final struggle resemble the official
myth of the "war to end war" dreamt up in 1914 by the allied

bourgeoisies. No period of transition; no dictatorship of the proletariat ("Down with all dictatorship!"); no repression after the workers' victory; no Revolutionary Tribunals; no Cheka! – above all, ye gods, no Cheka! – no more prisons . . . A smooth entry into the free city of communism, the arrival straight after the tempest at the Blessed Isles. What these revolutionaries – our libertarian brothers – prefer to the machine gun is garlands of roses, red roses.

A third lot, finally, profess that for the moment the monopoly of the use of the machine gun should be left to the possessing classes, and that one should try to lead them on gently, by persuasion, to give them up. Meanwhile, these reformers take infinite pains to get ultrarapid firing regulated by international conference. They appear to be divided into two categories: those who genuinely prefer negotiation to the machine gun; and those who, because they are practical and free from illusions, honestly prefer the use of asphyxiating gases.

In fact nobody – except perhaps a few manufacturers of arms and ammunition – has any special predilection for the machine gun. But the machine gun exists. It is a reality. Once the mobilization order goes out, you have the choice of being in front of it, or behind it: of serving the symbolic death machine, or being its target. We advise workers to turn to a third solution: to seize the instrument of murder and turn it against those who made it. The Russian Bolsheviks were saying from 1915: "Turn the imperialist war into civil war."

Everything we have just said about the machine gun applies to the state and its apparatus of constraint: prisons, courts, the police, the security services. The revolution does not have a choice of weapons. It amasses on its bloody arena those forged by history, those which have just fallen from the hands of a defeated ruling class. Yesterday, to constrain the exploited, the bourgeoisie had to use a heavy apparatus of coercion; today, to break the final resistance of the dispossessed exploiters, to stop them taking back the power, and then oblige them to abdicate their privileges for good, the proletariat and the peasantry require a powerful apparatus of repression. The machine gun does not disappear, it changes hands. There is no question of choosing the plowshare instead.

We should, however, be on guard against simplistic metaphors and analogies. It is not in the nature of the machine gun itself to change, whatever use is made of it. Whether it is muzzled with a cardboard plug and installed in a museum; whether it is used harmlessly in school training sessions; whether it is held by a plowman from Beauce cowering in a shell hole, to pierce the flesh of the Westphalian peasants who are his brothers; whether it is set up on the threshold of an expropriated palace, holding the counterrevolution at bay — not a thread, not a screw is changed.

An institution, on the contrary, does change along with the men and still more, infinitely more, the classes which make use of it. The army of the feudal monarchy before the French Revolution of 1789–93, a small full-time army, formed by paid mercenaries and poor devils recruited by force, and commanded by nobles, in no way resembles the army which comes after the bourgeois revolution, a nation in arms, spontaneously answering the call that "the fatherland is in danger" — an army commanded by former sergeants and by professional soldiers. Equally deep is the difference between the imperial army of the old regime in Russia, led to defeat by one Grand Duke Nicholas, with an officer caste, harshly imposed service and a "gagging" regime — and the Red Army organized by the Communist Party, with Trotsky as its great moving spirit, with its worker commissars, its propaganda services, its daily appeals to the class consciousness of the soldier, its epic victories. Equally deep, if not more so, is the difference between the bourgeois state, destroyed from top to bottom by the Russian Revolution of October 1917, and the proletarian state built on the rubble. We have raised the question of repression. We shall see that the analogy between the repressive apparatus of the bourgeois state and that of the proletarian state is much more apparent than real.

the experience
of two revolutions

In mid-November 1917, the soviets [workers' councils], exclusive holders of power for a few days, had carried a complete insurrectional victory throughout Russia, and now saw the era of difficulties opening up. To continue the revolution was going to be a hundred times more difficult for them than it had been to make it and take the power. In the big towns there was not a public service, or an administration working. The technicians' strike threatened the most densely populated towns with untold calamities. Water, electricity and provisions might run out in a few days; with the sewage works out of action, epidemics were to be expected; transport was more than a little precarious, and supplies were a problem. The first people's commissars

who came to take possession of the ministries found the
offices empty and closed up, with the cupboards locked,
and a few hostile, obsequious porters waiting for the new
masters to have the empty drawers of the secretaries forced
open. This sabotage by the bureaucracy and technicians,
organized by the capitalists (the "striking" civil servants got
a stipend from a committee of plutocrats), lasted for several
weeks at its sharpest, and for months, even years, in attenu-
ated form. Meanwhile the Civil War was slowly hotting
up. The victorious revolution, not the least inclined to shed
blood, in fact showed a dangerous degree of indulgence to its
enemies. Freed on parole (as in the case of General Krasnov),
or ignored, the monarchist officers assembled hastily in the
south, forming the first nuclei of the armies of Kornilov,
Alexeyev, Krasnov, Denikin and Wrangel. The magnanimity
of the young Soviet Republic was to cost her rivers of blood
for years. The historians will certainly ask themselves one
day—and communist theoreticians would undoubtedly do
well to keep ahead of the work of the historians—whether,
with greater rigor at the outset, with a dictatorship which
had been obliged to reduce the enemy classes to impotence
without delay by measures of public safety, even when these
classes may have appeared passive—whether Red Russia
could not in this way have spared herself something of the
horrors of civil war and the double terror of Red and White.
This was apparently Lenin's thinking, as he set himself very
early on to combat hesitations and half measures in repression, just as in everything else.

It was Trotsky's conception, spelled out in certain draconic
orders to the Red Army and in *Terrorism and Communism*. It
was Robespierre's pronouncement to the Convention on

January 16, 1792: "Clemency which makes pacts with tyranny is barbarous." The theoretical conclusion which seems to come out of the Russian experience is that a revolution cannot at its beginnings be either merciful, or indulgent, but must be harsh. In the class war, it is necessary to strike hard, and carry off decisive victories, so as not to have constantly to reconquer new ground, with constant new risks and new sacrifices.

Between October and December 1917, revolutionary justice carried out only 21 executions, the majority of them of social scum. The Extraordinary Commission for the Repression of Counterrevolution and Speculation, Cheka for short, was founded on December 7, in the face of increasingly bold operations by the enemy within. What was the situation at that point? In general outline, as follows:

The embassies and military missions of the Allies were centers of permanent conspiracy. Counterrevolutionaries of every hue there found subsidies, weapons, political direction. The industrialists, placed under workers' control, or dispossessed, were sabotaging production with the aid of the technicians. Tools, raw materials, stock, work secrets, everything which could be hidden was hidden, everything which could be stolen was stolen. The transport union and the co-ops, directed by the Mensheviks, aggravated the problem of supplies. Speculation made scarcity worse, and aggravated inflation.

The bourgeois Cadets (Constitutional Democrats) were conspiring; the Socialist Revolutionaries were conspiring; the Populists were conspiring; the Menshevik Social Democrats were conspiring; the anarchists were conspiring; the intellectuals were conspiring; the officers were conspiring; each

town had its secret chiefs of staff, its provisional governments, together with administrators and hangmen, ready
to emerge from the shadows after the imminent coup. It
was doubtful who could be rallied. On the Czechoslovak
front, the commander-in-chief of the Red Army, Muraviev,
was preparing to betray and go over to the enemy. The
Socialist Revolutionaries were preparing to assassinate
Lenin and Trotsky. Uritsky and Volodarsky were killed in
Petrograd. Nakhimson was killed in Yaroslavl. Uprising of
the Czechoslovaks; uprisings at Yaroslavl, Rybinsk, Murom,
Kazan . . . Plots by the Union for the Fatherland and Liberty;
plots by the Right Socialist Revolutionaries; attacks by
the Left Socialist Revolutionaries; the Lockhart affair (the
British acting consul in this case was less fortunate than M.
Noulens). Plots would follow one after the other for years,
undermining the state from within in line with the external
offensive of the White armies and foreign intervention. There
was to be the affair of the Tactical Center in Moscow; the
activities of the Englishman Paul Dukes and the Tagantsev
case in Petrograd; the attack by Leontievsky in Moscow (the
case of the "clandestine anarchists"); the betrayals of the
fort of Krasnaya-Gorka and the Semenovsky Regiment;[1]
the economic counterrevolution and speculation. For years,
directors of nationalized enterprises would in fact remain in
the service of the expropriated capitalists, giving them information, carrying out their orders, sabotaging production in
their interest; there would be countless abuses and excesses
of all kinds, the leading party would be infiltrated by those
who like to go fishing in troubled waters — mistakes by some,
corruption on the part of others; petty-bourgeois indivi-
dualism would be unleashed in chaotic struggles . . . There

was no question about the need for repression. The Cheka was no less indispensable than the Red Army and the Commissariat for Supplies.

A hundred and twenty years before, in a similar situation, the French Revolution had reacted in an almost identical manner. The revolutionaries of 1792 had their Committee of Public Safety, their Revolutionary Tribunal, Fouquier-Tinville, and the guillotine. Nor should we forget Jourdan the head chopper, or Carrier of Nantes.

The September days, the ban on émigrés, the law on suspects, the hunt for disaffected priests, the depopulation of the Vendée, the destruction of Lyon . . . "All internal enemies must be killed," Danton quite simply said, "in order to triumph over our external enemies." And accused before the Revolutionary Tribunal—he, the "minister of the revolution," of the September massacres, accused of wanting clemency—he cried out: "What does it matter if they call me the drinker of blood? Let us drink the blood of the enemies of humankind, if we have to . . ." I shall quote, not Marat, whom proletarian revolutionaries might with some reason claim to follow, but the great orator of the moderate party of the bourgeois revolution, Vergniaud. Requesting summary—terrorist—proceedings against the émigrés in the Legislative Assembly, on October 25, 1791, the tribune of the Gironde said:

> Legal proof! You count as nothing the blood this will cost you! Legal proof! Ah! We would rather avoid the disasters which would provide us with such proof!

By what strange aberration do the bourgeois of the Third Republic, whose ancestors used terror to defeat the monarchy, the nobility, the feudal clergy and foreign intervention, wax so indignant against the Red Terror?

terror has gone on for centuries

We do not deny that terror is terrible. Threatened with death, the proletarian revolution resorted to it in Russia for three years, from 1918 to 1921. It is too readily forgotten that apart from the revolutions necessary to give it birth, bourgeois society took centuries of terror to emerge and grow. Big capitalist property took shape over the centuries through the implacable eviction of the tillers of the soil; manufacturing and then industrial capital were accumulated by the implacable exploitation, aided by bloody legislation, of the dispossessed peasantry, reduced as they were to beggary.

This appalling page of history is passed over in silence in school textbooks and even in great works. We know of only one full account—concise but masterly—and that is by Karl Marx in Chapter 26 of *Capital*: "Primitive Accumulation." "At the end of the 15th and during the whole of the 16th century," Marx writes, "throughout Western Europe there was a bloody legislation against vagabondage. The fathers of the present working class were chastised for their enforced transformation into vagabonds and paupers." One of the aims of this very specific legislation was to supply industry with labor power. The lash was the sentence for vagrants, slavery for those who refused to work (Edward VI, King of England, decreed in 1547), branding with a red-hot iron for

those who tried to escape, and death for persistent offenders!
Theft was to be punished by death. According to Thomas
More, "7,200 great and petty thieves were put to death in the
reign of Henry VIII." England then had a population of three
to four million. "In Elizabeth's time, rogues were trussed
up apace, and there was not one year commonly wherein
three or four hundred were not devoured and eaten up by
the gallows." During this glorious reign, vagrants of over 18
whom nobody would hire for at least two years were put
to death. In France, "at the beginning of Louis XVI's reign
(ordinance of July 13th, 1777) every man in good health from
16 to 60 years of age, if without means of subsistence and
not practicing a trade, is to be sent to the galleys." In one of
her letters of which literary people are so fond, Madame de
Sévigné speaks with charming simplicity of the customary
hangings of peasants.

For centuries, justice has been nothing but terror organized
to the advantage of the possessing classes. To steal from a
rich man has always been a greater crime than to kill a poor
man. Since the falsification of history required by the class
interests of the bourgeoisie is the rule in the educational
systems of all democratic countries, so far as I know there is
still no serious history of social institutions in French at the
disposal of the schools, or the public. We are in fact obliged
to resort to documentation on Russia. The Marxist historian
M.N. Pokrovsky, in his remarkable *History of Russian Culture,*
devotes a chapter of some twenty pages to the subject of
justice. Under Ivan III, in the fifteenth century, justice was
administered by the *boyars,* the *dvoryane*—the nobility, the
privileged caste of landowners—and by "good" (meaning

more precisely by rich) peasants. The opinion of a few "good people" was more than enough to justify a death sentence, when, natu-rally, the accused was a poor man. "By the end of the 15th century," writes M.N. Pokrovsky, "it was already clear that the suppression of suspects was the essence of the law." Suspects to whom? To the rich, of course.

A document dating from 1539 confers the right of dispensing justice on the nobles (the *boyars*) assisted by "worthies" (rich peasants). The statute laid down the death penalty for "brigands whether caught in flagrante delicto, or not" and authorized the torturing of "bad people." Once the confession was obtained, the "guilty" party would be hanged; if he did not confess, he could still be imprisoned for life. The ordinances according this right did not admit that a nobleman could be put on trial; the law could only begin to be applied to peasants, merchants and craftsmen, and became rigorous only in the case of the poor. To grasp the ferocity of this justice, it is only necessary to go over the history of the peasant revolutions — the Peasant Wars in Germany, the "jacqueries" in France — which marked the emergence of capitalist property. Similar institutions existed in all countries where there was serfdom. This class justice of the feudal class of landowners did not completely disappear, giving way only gradually to the more complete but no less ferocious class justice of the absolute monarchies, characterized by the growing importance of commerce. Up until the bourgeois revolution — until the most recent period of history — there was no equality before justice, not even a purely formal equality, between rich and poor.

What is clear is that revolutions make no innovations in

the sphere of repression and terror; they only revive, in the form of emergency measures, the norms of law and justice which for centuries have been the weapons of the possessing classes against the dispossessed classes.

from Gallifet to Mussolini

Every time that social crises have raised the problem of repression, the modern bourgeoisie has not hesitated to revert to the most summary proceedings of class justice, treating its enemies as vagrants were treated in the fifteenth century. They were hanged; in 1848, the insurgent Parisians of the Saint-Antoine district — unemployed people, pushed over the brink by skilful provocation — were machine gunned in their thousands. We should never weary of recalling these great facts of history. The justification of the Red Terror was twice written by the bourgeoisie in advance, written in the finest human blood in history: by beheading the feudal aristocracy and two kings — Charles I of England (1649) and Louis XVI — in order to take the power; and by repressing proletarian uprisings. We can let the dates and facts speak for themselves for a moment.

The Paris Commune, in response to summary executions of its soldiers imprisoned by the Versaillais, shot 60 hostages. The Versaillais decimated the people of Paris. According to moderate estimates, the repression claimed more than 100,000 victims in Paris. Twenty thousand Communards, at least, were machine gunned to death, not in battle, but afterwards; 3,000 died in the prisons.

Did the Soviet Revolution in Finland, repressed in 1918 by the White Guards of Mannerheim in alliance with the German rearguard of von der Golz, strike some of its enemies before falling? Probably; but the number was so small that the bourgeoisie didn't even keep account of them. On the contrary, in this country of three-and-a-half million inhabitants, in which the proletariat is not a high proportion of the population, 11,000 workers were shot by the forces of law and order and more than 70,000 were interned in the concentration camps.

The Soviet Republic of Hungary (1919) was founded almost without bloodshed, thanks to the spontaneous abdication of the (bourgeois) government of Count Karolyi. When the People's Commissars of Budapest judged the situation desperate, they in turn abdicated, handing over power to the Social Democrats. For the three months that it lasted, the dictatorship of the Hungarian proletariat, though constantly threatened by internal plots and by the Czechoslovak and Romanian invasions across its frontiers, killed a total of 350 of its enemies — including the counterrevolutionaries who fell, arms in hand, in local uprisings. Horthy's courts and officer gangs killed thousands of people in "reprisals" and interned, imprisoned and maimed tens of thousands.

The Munich Soviet (1919), in response to the massacre of 23 Red prisoners by the "regular" army, shot 12 hostages. After the Reichswehr entered Munich, 505 people were shot in the town, 321 of them without the slightest pretence of justice. This number included some 60 Russians picked up by chance.

There are no valid statistics on the victims of the White Terror in Russia in the areas where counterrevolution and foreign intervention triumphed. But the victims of the anti-Semitic pogroms in the Ukraine alone, under General Denikin, are estimated at one million. The Jewish population of whole towns (such as Fastov) was systematically wiped out.

The number of workers who died in the repression of workers' insurrections in Germany, from 1918 to 1921, was estimated at 15,000.

I shall not record here either the names of martyrs, or symbolic episodes. I am only trying quickly to give certain principles a grounding in fact. On this point there have been too many painful experiences from which the proletariat should have learned. Too many dictatorships and too many White Terror regimes are still in operation for detailed examples to be necessary.

From Gallifet to Mussolini, via Noske, the repression of revolutionary proletarian movements, even when accepted and presided over by social democrats, as happened in Germany, is characterized by the evident determination to strike at the living strength of the laboring classes; in other words to physically exterminate the leaderships as far as possible.

bourgeois law
and proletarian law

Repression is one of the essential functions of all political power. The revolutionary state, at least in the first phase of its existence, needs it more than any other. It appears that in its three basic elements — the police, the army, the courts and prisons — the mechanism of repression and coercion does not vary. We have just made a study of a secret police force. We have gone into its most secret recesses and dirtiest corners. And we have seen its impotence. In the hands of the *ancien régime*, as we said, this weapon could neither save it nor destroy the revolution. We do, however, admit the decisive efficacy of this same weapon in the hands of the revolution. The weapon is only the same in appearance; an institution, we repeat, undergoes profound transformation according to the class it serves and the ends it pursues.

From top to bottom, the Russian Revolution destroyed the coercive apparatus of the *ancien régime*. On these ruins, it triumphantly built its own apparatus of force.

Let us now endeavor to outline the basic differences between repression as exercised by the capitalist class and repression as exercised by the revolutionary class. From the general principles, which a summary analysis will reveal to us, will be deduced some corollaries on the role of the police in each case.

In bourgeois society, power is exercised by rich minorities against poor majorities. A government is only ever an executive committee of an oligarchy of financiers supported by the privileged classes. Legislation aimed at maintaining in obedience all the wage workers — the majority of the population — must of necessity be very complex and very severe. Every serious attack on property must in one way or another result in the suppression of the guilty party. Thieves are no longer hanged, not because "humanitarian principles" are "making progress," but because the balance of forces between the possessing classes and the non-possessing classes

and the development of class consciousness among the poor
no longer permit the judge to throw such insults at the poor.
But—and we are only speaking of French law, which is of
only medium ferocity—major theft is punished by forced
labor; and the sentence of forced labor is carried out in such
circumstances and with such "supplementary conditions"
that the life of the convict is certain to be broken. Every
sentence of five years' hard labor means a double sentence:
once set free, the prisoner is obliged to remain in the colonies
for a period equal to his stay in prison; those sentenced to
more than eight years' hard labor are condemned to stay
in Guyana for life. This is the most unhealthy of the French
colonies! Banishment, the "supplementary" life sentence,
also means Guyana, and is very close to being forced labor.
It is the lot above all of repeat offenders in nonprofessional
crime. Four sentences of theft, larceny, etc.—the successive
theft of four 100-sous coins would be a case in point, and
I have leafed through enough criminal files to know that
this is the kind of case at issue—can lead to banishment. Or
seven sentences for vagrancy. In other words, to be found
on seven successive occasions on the streets of Paris with
no bread and no roof over your head is a crime punishable
by a life sentence. In England and Belgium, where there are
workhouses and *dépôts de mendicité* (beggars' centers), the repression of begging and vagrancy is no less implacable. One
more thing: the bosses have need of manpower and cannon
fodder so the law punishes abortion implacably.

The eternal nature of private property and wage labor
being taken for granted at the outset, no effective remedy can
be applied to social ills such as crime. A permanent battle is
on between order and crime, "the army of crime," army of

the poor, the army of the victims, of the irresponsible, who are pointlessly and indefinitely decimated. The point has still not been made clearly enough that the struggle against crime is an aspect of the class struggle. At least three quarters of common law criminals belong to the exploited classes.

The penal code of the proletarian state does not, as a general rule, allow the death penalty in criminal cases (except sometimes where the physical suppression of particular incurable, dangerous lunatics is the only solution). Nor does it allow life sentences. The severest sentence is 10 years' imprisonment. Deprivation of liberty, a measure taken for the safety of society and for reeducation, is conceived of as excluding the medieval idea of punishment, of suffering imposed by way of expiation. In this realm, and in the present situation of the Soviet Union, the material possibilities are naturally far behind the goal. The building of the new society — which will be without prisons — does not begin with the construction of ideal prisons. This is beyond doubt; but the impulse is there, and a thorough reform has begun. Like the legislature, the courts, from the clearest class standpoint, take account of the social causes of crime, and the social origins and situation of the criminal. Being without bread, or lodging, as we have seen, is a serious crime in Paris; in Moscow it is, in a criminal case, an important mitigating circumstance.

Under bourgeois law, to be poor is often a crime, and always an aggravating circumstance or ground for presuming guilt. Under proletarian law, to be rich — even within the very strict limits in which, during the period of the New Economic Policy (NEP), individual enrichment is tolerated — is always an aggravating circumstance.

two systems

The great liberal doctrine of the state from which the capitalist rulers have only really deviated in wartime — when they had their own war capitalism, characterized by state control of production, strict control of trade and of the distribution of products (with rationing cards), a state of emergency, etc. — advocates the noninterference of the state in economic life. In political economy it adheres to the laissez-faire/ laissez-passer position of the Manchester school. The state is considered to be the instrument for the collective defense of the possessing classes; a war machine against competing national groups, a machine for repressing the exploited. The administrative functions of the state are reduced to a minimum; it is under the influence of socialism and the pressure of the masses that the modern state not so long ago took over the management of public education. The economic functions of the state are reduced, as far as possible, to the establishment of customs tariffs aimed at protecting industrialists against foreign competition. (Labor legislation is always a gain of the workers' movement.) In a word, respect for capitalist anarchy is the rule for the state. Whether you produce, sell, resell, speculate without limit, with no concern for the general interest: it's all right. Competition is the law of the market. Crises thus become the great regulators of economic life; they rectify the errors of the big industrialists at the expense of the workers, the lower middle classes and the weakest capitalists. Even when big trusts ruling over whole countries effectively suppress competition in vast spheres of production and trade, the old doctrine of the state, so much in line with the interests of the kings of steel, coal, salt pork, or shipping, remains generally untouched; such is the case in the United States.

This recollection of facts which everybody should know is obligatory for us in order to make a better definition of the workers' and peasants' state, as in the Soviet Union, with its nationalization of the land, minerals, transport, large-scale industry and foreign trade. The soviet state governs economic life. It acts each day directly in the essential functions of economic life. Within the narrow limits in which it permits capitalist initiative, it controls and regulates it, exercising a double tutelage over it: by law and by what we may call direct action on the market, credit and production. The prevention of crises is one of the most characteristic features of the policy of the soviet state. Every effort is made to eliminate crises from the time the first symptoms appear; it is not unreasonable to predict, once social development has reached a certain point, that they can be completely eliminated.

Whereas the capitalist state is content on principle only to fight the ultimate effects of social causes it does not permit itself to tackle, the soviet state takes action on these causes. Begging, prostitution, the precarious state of public health, crime, the decline of the population and the low birth rate,[2] are only the effects of deep-lying economic causes. After each economic crisis, crime increases; it can't be otherwise. And the capitalist courts become doubly severe. For the troubles caused by the normal working of the capitalist economy — anarchic, irrational, governed by the egoism of individuals and by the collective egoism of the possessing classes — the bourgeoisie knows no remedy but repression.[3] The soviet state, attacking the causes of the evil, has evidently much less need of repression. The more it develops, the more efficient, concerted and planned will be its economic activity, the less repression will be necessary, until the day when the intelligent management of production will, through prosperity, suppress social ills such as crime—which has to be dealt with by coercion in order to prevent the spread of the infection. There will be much less thieving when no one is hungry any longer; there will be no thieving at all once abundance for all is accomplished.

Even today—and we are a long way from our goal!—our conviction is that, contrary to appearances, the soviet state uses infinitely less repression than any other. Just think about it: in the present economic situation of Russia, would a bourgeois government not have to rule by force to an infinitely greater extent than the soviets? The peasantry are often discontented. They find the taxes too high and industrial articles too dear. Their discontent is sometimes expressed in acts which have to be classed as counterrevolutionary. The peasantry as a whole has nonetheless given the soviets the military victory—the Red Army consisted above all of peasants—and continues to support them. A capitalist government, restoring the land to the landowners, would have had to contain the anger of a hundred million peasants, which it could only have done by unceasing, pitiless repression. This is precisely why all the White regimes in the pay of foreign financial interests have fallen.

In its present bereft state, after years of imperialist war, civil war, blockades and famine, encircled by capitalist states, the target for financial blockades, diplomatic intrigues and war preparations, the Soviet Union, still an entrenched camp besieged by the enemy and moreover grappling with the internal contradictions inherent in such a difficult period of transition, still has great need of repression. It would be excessively self-deluding to think that the period of counter-revolutionary attacks is over. But whatever the present difficulties of the Soviet Union and the way it reacts to them, the essential features of the soviet state are not changed by them—nor, therefore, is the role played by repression.

economic constraints: hunger

It is moreover too often forgotten that soviet society, in its eighth year of existence, cannot be fairly compared to bourgeois society, which has the advantage of a tradition of authority several centuries old and more than a century of political experience. Long before 1789, the Third Estate was, contrary to Sièyes's vehement claim, a respected force within the state. The first fifty years of economic development of the bourgeoisie were no less years of atrocious class dictatorship for that. The falsifiers of official history knowingly willed into oblivion the truth about the first half of the 19th century. Modern capitalism, marching on to opulence, rode over the bodies of several generations of workers who lived in hovels, slaved from dawn to dusk, had no democratic rights, and gave over their eight-year-old children to the factory, to be devoured down to the very muscles. On the bones, flesh, blood and sweat of the generations thus sacrificed the whole of modern civilization was built. Bourgeois science ignores them. We are obliged to refer the reader to Karl Marx's *Capital*. He will find in Chapter 23 terrible pages on England from 1846 to 1866. I cannot resist quoting a few lines from it. A doctor, charged with making an official inquiry, finds that "indeed, as regards the indoor operatives, the work which obtains the scanty pittance of food, is for the most part excessively prolonged. Yet evidently it is only in a qualified sense that the work can be deemed self-supporting." Another investigator says there are "about 20 large colonies in London, of about 10,000 persons each, whose miserable condition exceeds almost anything he has seen elsewhere in England." "Newcastle-upon-Tyne," says Dr. Hunter, "contains a sample of the finest tribe of our countrymen, often sunk by external circumstances of house and street into an almost savage degradation." The *Standard*, an English conservative paper, wrote on April 5, 1866, in relation to the jobless of London: "Let us remember what these people suffer. They are dying of hunger . . . There are 40,000 of them . . . In our presence, in one quarter of this wonderful metropolis, are packed — next door to the most enormous accumulation of wealth the world ever saw — cheek by jowl with this are 40,000 helpless, starving people." "The Irish famine of 1846 killed more than 1,000,000 people . . . To the wealth of the country, it did not the slightest damage." (K. Marx)

To transform the sweat and blood of these wretched people into ringing guineas of full weight, bearing the portrait of Queen Victoria; for these hopeless people, condemned by the development of machinery and crises, to die in poverty, to consent to die without revolt, like shackled beasts, what formidable constraint was required? But one of the principal means of capitalist constraint is clearly in evidence: hunger. It was half a century of what could be called economic terror. The worker labored, threatened with unemployment, threatened with dying of hunger, labored like an industrial galley slave, labored like a beast, only to die of hunger in the end — after fifteen short years. (We have no data on the average life expectancy of wageworkers at this period, which is regrettable; such figures would sum the whole thing up.) It is still the same in our day: economic constraint — by means of hunger — is by far the most important factor, and the only really effective one, while repression only adds to it what is required to defend capitalist "order" against certain particularly worrying categories of its victims (thieves) and against revolutionaries.

decimation, mistakes and abuses

To repeat: terror is terrible. In civil war, for every fighter — and such wars scarcely admit of any neutral parties — it is a question of life, or death. Educated in the schools of the reactionaries, the working class, living under the shadow of the threat to its life, must strike its enemies to death. Prison intimidates no one; riots too easily break down the bolted doors which can also be opened by corruption, or the ingenuity of conspirators.

Another necessity arises at the most intense point of the struggle, to resort to the ravages of terror. From the time of the armies of ancient days, decimation is the classic way of keeping troops in obedience. It was practiced during the Great War, notably on the French front after the mutinies of April 1917. This should not be forgotten. It involves executing one man in ten, without concern for the guilt, or innocence of the individual. On this point, a historical observation is in order. In 1871, the Communards were more than decimated by the Versaillais. We have already quoted the moderate estimate of the number shot by Gallifet: 20,000. The Commune had 160,000 fighters. The redoubtable logic of class war — that is what the French bourgeoisie, the most enlightened in the world, the bourgeoisie of Taine and Renan! — teaches us with these figures. A class does not admit itself to be defeated, a class is not conquered, until such a high percentage of losses is inflicted on it. Imagine — a situation familiar in Russia in the heroic years of the revolution — a town of 100,000 inhabitants divided into 70,000 proletarians (I am simplifying: proletarians and related elements) and 30,000 people belonging to the bourgeoisie and the middle class, accustomed to considering themselves as forming the legitimate ruling class, educated and not lacking in material means. Is it not obvious, especially if the struggle is limited to the town, that the resistance of this counterrevolutionary force, however strongly or weakly organized, will not be broken until it has suffered some quite impressive losses? And is it not less dangerous for the revolution to strike too hard than not to strike hard enough?

The bourgeoisie has furnished the exploited classes with plenty of bloody warnings. Now they are rebounding on it. History warns of this: the more suffering and poverty they inflict on the laboring classes, the more bitterly they resist the day of reckoning, the more dearly will they pay.

Like the Revolutionary Tribunal of the French Revolution, but in general with rather less summary proceedings, the

Cheka of the Russian Revolution dealt out justice to its class enemies, implacably and without the right of appeal; like the Revolutionary Tribunal, it judged less on the basis of depositions and precise charges and more on the enemy's social origins, political attitude, outlook and ability to do damage. It was much more a question of striking a class through those belonging to it, than weighing up definite acts. Class justice only dwells on the examination of individual cases in periods of calm.

Mistakes, abuses and excesses appear particularly disastrous in relation to social layers which the proletariat must seek to rally to it: the middle peasantry, lower layers of the middle classes, intellectuals with no private means; and also in relation to dissidents of the revolution, sincere revolutionaries who take up objectively counterrevolutionary positions because of ideologies far removed from an understanding of the realities of the revolution. I remember the anarchists who, in 1920, when the Red Fleet was defending Kronstadt and Petrograd with difficulty against an English attack, regardless went on in their few boats with their old antimilitarist propaganda. I am also thinking of the Left Socialist Revolutionaries who, in 1918, sought to throw the Soviet Republic, deprived of an army and of any kind of resources, into a new war against German imperialism, which was still strong. Between these "revolutionaries" gone astray and the men of the old regime, revolutionary repression endeavored and must always endeavor to distinguish; but it is not always possible.

In every social battle, a certain percentage of excesses, abuses and errors cannot be avoided. The duty of the party and of all revolutionaries is to work to limit these. The scale of these errors only really depends on the following factors:

- The balance of forces at the time and the bitterness of the struggle
- The level of organization of the action; the effectiveness of control over the action exercised by the party of the proletariat
- The level of culture of the proletarian and peasant masses

A certain cruelty results from the material circumstances of the struggle; full to overflowing, the prisons of a proletarian revolution do not, in respect of hygiene, bear comparison with the bourgeoisie's "good prisons" in normal times. In besieged cities where famine and typhus rule, there are rather more deaths from this in prison than outside. What is to be done about it? When the jail is full of proletarians and peasants, this idle question does not bother the philanthropists in the slightest. At the time the Communard prisoners were held in the Satory camp, lying under the open sky on the bare ground, in the mud, shivering through terrible nights in pouring rain—forbidden to get up, and the sentinels with orders to shoot at anyone who did get up—a great philosopher, Taine, wrote: "These wretches have put themselves beyond the bounds of humanity . . ."

Following the seizure of power, the proletariat, called to tasks without number, firstly resolves the more important: food supplies, city organization, external and internal defense, the inventory of expropriated goods, the seizure of wealth. It devotes its best forces to them. Revolutionary repression—and this is a cause of mistakes and abuses—is left only with second-rate personnel, albeit under leaders who absolutely must be taken from among the firmest and finest of men. (This is what the dictatorship of the proletariat did in Russia, with Dzherzhinsky — and in Hungary, with Otto Corvin.) The tasks of internally defending a revolution are often among the most delicate, the most painful and sometimes the most horrific. Some of the best of the revolutionaries — men of high conscience, scrupulous outlook and unswerving character — must devote themselves to it.

Through their intervention the party exercises its control. This political and moral control — unceasing in this field as in every other — expresses both the intervention of the most conscious vanguard of the working class, and the scarcely less direct intervention of the masses of the people under the effective control of whom the party is situated in every action it takes. This guarantees the class character of the repression. The possibilities of mistakes and abuses are reduced in proportion to the forces which the vanguard of the proletariat is able to put into this sector.

repression and provocation

In the course of our study of the Okhrana we dwelt a long time on provocation. It is not a necessary technique for every police force. The task of a police force is to carry out surveillance, to get to know, to prevent; not to provoke, activate and incite. In bourgeois states, police provocation, scarcely known in periods of strength, acquires growing importance in proportion as the regime declines, is weakened and slides into the abyss. The present situation should be enough to convince us. Practically insignificant at this point in the workers' movement in France, Belgium and England, countries of relative prosperity for capitalism, in Germany, following the revolutionary crisis of late 1923, provocation was no less important than in Russia, after the defeated revolution of 1905. The Leipzig trial of April-March 1925, known as the trial of the German "Cheka," in which the Berlin police carried out a nighttime raid on one of the defendants, Kurt Rosenfeld, reveals that the workings of the secret police of the Reich are very similar to those of the former Okhrana. In another country, where reaction has for almost two years been struggling with a popular revolution — Bulgaria — the same phenomenon occurs, but it is still more accentuated. In Poland, provocation has become the weapon par excellence of reaction against the workers' movement. These are examples enough.

Police provocation is above all the weapon — or the curse — of decomposing regimes. Conscious of their impotence to prevent what is going on, the police incite initiatives which they then repress. Provocation is also a spontaneous, elementary action, resulting from the demoralization of a police force at its wits' end, overtaken by events, which cannot perform a task infinitely above its capacities, and nonetheless wants to justify the expectations and expenditures of its masters.

when is repression effective?

The Okhrana was unable to prevent the fall of the autocracy. But the Cheka made a strong contribution to preventing the overthrow of soviet power.

The Russian autocracy, in fact, fell rather than being overthrown. A shaking was all it took. The old, dilapidated building, whose demolition was wished for by the great majority of the population, came tumbling down. The economic development of Russia meant the revolution was required. What could the secret police do about it? Was it up to them to solve the conflict of interests of the opposing camps of deadly enemies, desperate to escape from a situation with no way out other than the class war—the industrial and financial bourgeoisie, big landlords, the nobility, the intellectuals, the *déclassé*, the proletariat, the peasant masses? Their actions could only gain the *ancien régime* a limited reprieve, and that on condition that it agreed to certain appropriate measures of general policy. How absurd was this thin line of policemen and agents provocateurs, working blindly to turn back the beating of the waves against the old, cracked, shaking cliff, ready to crumble and engulf them!

The functions of the Cheka are not so absurd. In a country divided between Red and White, in which the Red are naturally the majority, it seeks out the enemy, discovers them and strikes. It is no more than a weapon, in the hands of the majority, against the minority—one weapon among many others, and a supplementary one at that. It only takes on major importance because of the danger that the enemy's bullets may strike the revolution in the head. It is said that the day after the seizure of power, Lenin worked all night on the decree for the expropriation of the land. "As long," he said, "as we have the time to get it through — let them try to take it from us after that!" The expropriation of the lands of the nobility instantly procured the support of 100 million peasants for the Bolsheviks.

Repression is effective when it completes the effect of efficient measures of general policy. Before the October Revolution, when Kerensky's cabinet refused to satisfy the demands of the peasantry, the arrest of revolutionary agitators only increased trouble and exasperation in the villages. After the displacement of social forces which took place in the countryside through the expropriation of the land, the interests of the peasantry led them to defend soviet power, and the arrest of Socialist Revolutionary, or monarchist agitators — the former trying to exploit their past popularity in the countryside, the latter to play on religious feelings — removed one cause of disturbance.

Repression is an effective weapon in the hands of an energetic class, conscious of what it wants, and serving the interests of the greatest number. In the hands of a degenerate aristocracy, whose privileges are an obstacle to the economic development of society, it is historically ineffective. Let us not deny that it can be as useful to a strong bourgeoisie in decisive periods as to the proletariat during the Civil War.

Repression is effective when it acts along the lines of historical development; it is impotent in the last reckoning when it goes against the grain of historical development.

consciousness of the dangers and the goal

On twenty occasions, at the height of the Civil War as before the seizure of power, Lenin occupied himself with reestablishing Marx's teaching on the disappearance of the state and the final abolition of constraint in communist society. One of the reasons he invokes when calling for the replacement of the word "social-democrat" by "communist" in the name of the Bolshevik Party is that "the term social-democrat is scientifically inaccurate. Democracy is one of the forms of the state. Now, as Marxists, we are against all states."[4] I can also recall an article he wrote, in bitter days, for May 1 (in 1920, I believe). The iron fist of the proletarian party was still keeping War Communism going. The Red Terror was only somewhat abated. Beyond the heroic, terrible present, the men and women of the revolution kept their eyes calmly fixed on the goal. Immune to any utopianism, scornful of dreamers but unshakably attached to pursuing the basic aims of the revolution, Lenin, the uncontested leader of the first proletarian state, the moving spirit of a dictatorship, would evoke the future in which work and the distribution of its products will be governed by the rule "from each according to their ability, to each according to their need."

Here is the supreme difference between the capitalist state and the proletarian state: the workers' state works for its own disappearance. The supreme difference marked by the constraint-repression exercised by the dictatorship of the proletariat, is that the latter constitutes a necessary class weapon working for the abolition of all constraint.

That must never be forgotten. This consciousness of the highest goals is also a force.

At the end of the last century, it was possible to entertain the great dream of an idyllic social transformation. Broad-minded people went in for this, scorning, or twisting Marx's science. They dreamed of the social revolution as the virtually painless expropriation of a tiny minority of plutocrats. Why should the proletariat in its magnanimity not break up the old blades and the modern firearms and grant an indemnity to its exploiters of yesterday? The last of the rich would peaceably die out, at leisure, surrounded by an atmosphere of healthy distrust. The expropriation of the treasures accumulated by capitalists, together with the rational reorganization of production, would instantly procure well-being and security for the whole of society. All prewar working class ideologies were to some degree penetrated by these false ideas. The radical myth of progress dominated. The imperialist powers were nonetheless mounting their artillery. In the Second International, a handful of revolutionary Marxists alone discerned the great outlines of historical development. In France, on the question of proletarian violence, some revolutionary syndicalists had a clear view of things.

Capitalism, previously no doubt iniquitous and cruel but wealth creating, now, in the apogee of its history which began on August 2, 1914, became the destroyer of its own civilization, the exterminator of its own peoples. After its prodigious development throughout a century of discoveries and feverish advances, scientific technique, in the hands of the big bourgeois, the bankers and the trusts, was turned against humanity. Everything of use for production and for extending human beings' power over nature and enriching life was now used to destroy and kill with suddenly heightened powers. A morning's bombing was enough to destroy a city, the work of centuries of culture. One six-millimeter bullet was enough to cut short the working of the best-organized brain. We cannot forget that a new imperialist conflagration could mortally wound European civilization, which has already been so hard hit. It is fair enough to predict that due to the advance of "military art," we shall see the depopulation of whole countries by air forces armed with the chemical weapons whose unnamed dangers were denounced in 1924 in an official document by the League of Nations — whom no one will accuse of revolutionary demagogy! The flesh and bones of the millions of dead of 1914-18, under their patriotic monuments, were still not enough to remove this threat from humankind. Looking the harsh realities of revolution in the face, we must not forget these things. The sacrifices imposed by the Civil War, the implacable necessity for terror, the rigors of revolutionary repression, and the inevitability of painful mistakes, then appear in their rightful proportions. They are the smallest of evils compared with such immense calamities. The cemetery of Verdun alone would be more than enough to justify them.

"Revolution or Death." This watchword from a fighter at Verdun[5] still contains profound truth. In the coming dark hours of history, this will be the dilemma. The time will have arrived for the working class to carry out the harsh but salutary, saving task: the revolution.

notes

Introduction

1. Victor Serge, *Memoirs of a Revolutionary* (New York: Writers & Readers Publishers, 1984).
2. Victor Serge, *Memoirs of a Revolutionary*.
3. Victor Serge, *Memoirs of a Revolutionary*.
4. Susan Weissman, *Victor Serge: The Course is Set on Hope* (London/ NewYork: Verso, 2001).
5. Victor Serge, *Memoirs of a Revolutionary*.
6. Nadin Hamoui, "Justice For All: Selective Enforcement in a Post-9/11 Era," June 4, 2003, at Washington D.C.
7. Mako Nakagawa, "Justice For All: Selective Enforcement in a Post-9/11 Era," June 4, 2003, at Washington D.C.
8. Victor Serge, *The Long Dusk*, with credit to Susan Weissman, *Victor Serge: The Course is Set on Hope* for calling it to my attention.

1. The Russian Okhrana

1. Conversely, individual or collective initiatives in line with the needs and aspirations of the party — that is, of the proletariat — acquire their greatest effectiveness within it.
2. I. Kaliaev, on the orders of the Socialist Revolutionary Party, executed Grand Duke Sergei (in Moscow in 1905) and was hanged. Igor Sazonov, in the same year, executed the government minister Plehve, in Saint Petersburg. Condemned to death, pardoned, sent to do forced labor, and then amnestied, he committed suicide in Akatui Prison a few months before his sentence was due to expire, as a protest against the mistreatment of his fellow prisoners. These two men, of high moral standing, left deep-rooted memories in Russia.
3. Stolypin, the head of the czar's government in the period of implacable reaction following the 1905 revolution, devoted himself to consolidating the regime by means of systematic repression and agrarian reform.
4. Few in number, the Maximalists, dissidents from the Socialist Revolutionary Party, reproaching it for the corruption of its leaders and opportunist ideology, were primarily intrepid terrorists, though their theories were radical to the point of fantasy. There still are a handful of them, closely bound up with the Left Socialist Revolutionaries.
5. Solomon Ryss was to pay dearly for his boldness. Arrested in the south of Russia, after some risky actions, he had to defend himself, before the judges, against the terrible suspicions of his comrades in arms, refused to go back on "active service" with the Okhrana, and on being sentenced to death, died like a revolutionary.

6. M. Raymond Recouly still proclaims his unqualified patriotism in the bourgeois papers . . . But then, money has no smell.

7. Haase was a leader of German Social Democracy killed by a madman in 1919; Dan was a Russian Menshevik.

8. Close collaboration is almost the rule in relations between the police forces of the capitalist states, so that in one sense you can speak of an international police. Concerning the beginnings of collaboration between the czarist Okhrana and the Political Police of the Third Republic in France, see the curious, detailed account contained in an old book by Ernest Daudet, *Histoire diplomatique de l'alliance franco-russe* (1894). This shows how the then ministers, Freyssinet, Ribot and Constant, connived with the Russian ambassador, Morenheim, to procure the arrest of a group of nihilists, who were moreover organized by the informer Landesen (who later, under the name of Harting, rose to a diplomatic career in France, receiving the Legion of Honor). Another equally neglected book, *L'alliance franco-russe*, by Jules Hansen, confirms this version. Finally, the former security chief, Goron, tells in his memoirs of how the prefect of Paris asked the Russian police chief in Paris (Rachkovsky) for the collaboration of his agents in keeping watch on certain emigrants (quoted by V. Burtzev). We note these avowals in spite of their date; the authors are above any suspicion of intention to slander the French government.

   We should refer here to much more recent events which unfortunately have not made the headlines as they should have, even in the labor press. In February 1922, Nicolau Fort, one of the supposed assassins of the Spanish minister, Dato, and his companion Joaquina Concepcion, was handed over by the German police to the Spanish police, via the French police. The handover of the extradited prisoners took place under the greatest secrecy. The Spanish government paid a substantial reward to the Berlin police. In 1925, under the Herriot government, the French constabulary and police on the Pyrenees frontier on different occasions refused entry to Spanish workers being hunted by Primo de Rivera's police.

9. A writer and a liberal, Vladimir Burtzev devoted himself to the history of the revolutionary movement and the fight against police provocation. He unmasked Azev, Harting-Landesen, and many other provocateurs. He advocated individual terrorism against the *ancien régime*. After the fall of czarism, he, like the majority of the Socialist Revolutionaries, moved rapidly towards the counterrevolution. A friend and colleague of G. Hervé, who favored intervention in Russia, he was to become a propagandist for Denikin, Kolchak and Wrangel in Paris.

10. The whole of the correspondence between this individual and his superiors is highly instructive. We see the head of security in Saint Petersburg assuring Krassilnikov that the Russian authorities will in any circumstances deny his role in the Russian police; we see this strange "embassy adviser" (his official title) machinating an extraordinarily complicated intrigue to derail Burtzev's inquiries. An ex-foreign agent of the Russian police, Jollivet, enters into contact with Burtzev, makes revelations to him and undertakes to keep watch on someone suspected as a provocateur, but in reality he is watching Burtzev himself and informing on him to the Okhrana. Informing and betrayal to the third degree! A maze of intrigue . . .

11. Byloe, *Le Passé* (Paris: 1908).
12. The file on surveillance of the social-democratic organizations, for the year 1912 alone, amounts to 250 thick volumes.
13. It later became a patriotic, governmental party, full of police — Pilsudski's party.
14. *Konspirativno?*
15. The carpenter Stepan Khalturin, who in 1878 founded the Southern Union of Russian Workers, was one of the real precursors of the Russian labor movement. A quarter of a century before his time, he conceived that the revolution could be carried out through a general strike. Getting a job as a carpenter among the staff at the Winter Palace, he slept for a long time on a mattress he gradually filled up with dynamite . . . Alexander II escaped the explosion of February 5, 1880. Khalturin was hanged two years later, after executing the Kiev prosecutor, Strelnikov. He had been driven into terrorism by the police provocation which dissolved his group of workers. He is one of the finest and most noble figures of the history of the Russian Revolution.
16. Kerensky's democratic republic thought it could protect them, and managed to get a few of them abroad.

2. The problem of illegality
1. A circular from Minister Jarres, in 1924, authorized the state forces to hound and arrest all revolutionary workers. It is a known fact that this led to the arrest of about 7,000 communists.
2. The Yugoslav Communist Party reorganized in illegality. It now has several thousand members.
3. See V.I. Lenin, *What Is To Be Done?*
4. Jean Maxe was identified by the magazine *Les Humbles*. He was one Jean Didier, resident in Paris (28th arrondissement). To tell the truth, his laborious compilations on the Clartist-Judeo-Germanic-Bolshevik plot (!) are more like cheap thrillers than serious police investigations. However, the French bourgeoisie appreciated them.
5. See S. Howard and Robert W. Dunn, "The Labor Spy," in *The New Republic* (New York); and the novel by Upton Sinclair, *100%: The Story of a Patriot.*
6. Henceforth in the great capitalist countries, every war will tend to turn more and more into a domestic class war. To militarize industry and place the whole nation on a war alert requires first that the revolutionary workers' movement be crushed. I have attempted to show, in a series of articles on the coming war, that militarization will mean a strangling of the workers' movement as quickly as possible. Only parties, unions and organizations which have prepared for it will survive this blow. It would be wise to make a thorough investigation of these questions.

3. Simple advice to revolutionaries
1. When Igor Sazonov planted his bomb under von Plehve's carriage (Petersburg, 1905), the minister was killed and the terrorist seriously injured. When they took him to the hospital, the wounded man was surrounded by skilled spies, who were ordered to take down every word he uttered in his delirium. As soon as Sazonov recovered consciousness, he was brutally interrogated. From prison he wrote to his comrades:

"Remember that the enemy is infinitely vile!" The Okhrana even had the audacity to send false lawyers to the accused.

4. The problem of revolutionary repression

1. I have given an account of these episodes in *Pendant la guerre civile* (During the Civil War), (Paris: Librairie du Travail, 1921).

2. The decline in the birth rate worries the leaders of the French bourgeoisie considerably. The commissions set up to study the reasons for it have quite correctly come to the conclusion that this is a phenomenon characteristic of a country of smallholders. What then can the legislator do? All he is able to do is to deliver platonic admonitions to the self-centered smallholder, who wants only one child.

3. I have already referred elsewhere to the days of June 1848. The oblivion into which this glorious and uplifting page of the history of the French proletariat has passed is much to be regretted. The bourgeoisie of the Second Republic were undergoing a crisis, resulting in a rise in unemployment. They found only one solution to the unemployment problem: to provoke an uprising and then suppress it. Paul-Louis, in his *Histoire du socialisme français*, gives a concise picture of these events.

4. See V. Serge, *Lenine, 1917* (Paris: Librairie du Travail, 1925).

5. Raymond Lefebvre.